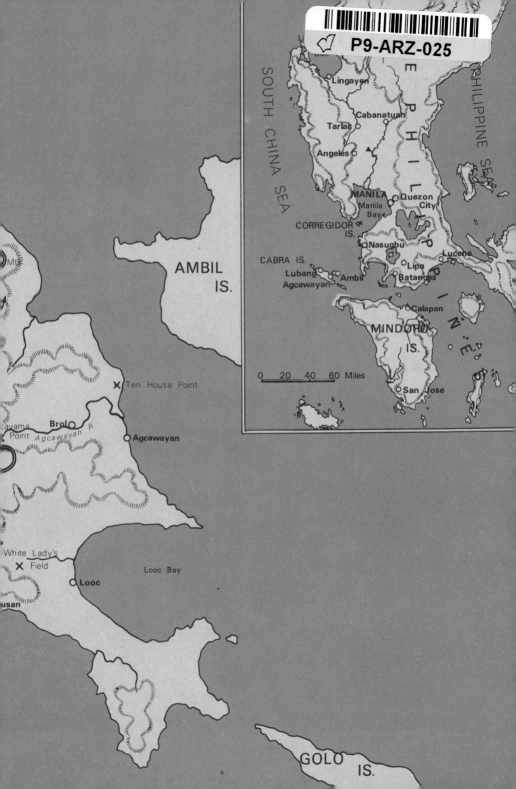

SOUTH CHINA SEA

PHILIPPINE SEA

Lingayen

Cabanatuan

Tarlac

Angeles

MANILA
Manila Bay
Quezon City

CORREGIDOR IS.

Nasugbu

CABRA IS.

Lubang
Agcawayan
Ambil

Lipe
Batangas

Lucena

Calapan

MINDORO IS.

0   20   40   60 Miles

San Jose

AMBIL IS.

Mt.

× Ten House Point

Brol

ayama
Point *Agcawayan* R.

Agcawayan

White Lady's
× Field

Looc Bay

Looc

usan

GOLO IS.

Max Kelson

NO SURRENDER

HIROO ONODA

NO SURRENDER

MY THIRTY-YEAR WAR

Translated by
CHARLES S. TERRY

KODANSHA INTERNATIONAL LTD.
TOKYO, NEW YORK & SAN FRANCISCO

Distributors:

UNITED STATES: Harper & Row, Publishers, Inc.
10 East 53rd Street, New York, New York 10022
SOUTH AMERICA: Harper & Row, International Department

CANADA: Fitzhenry & Whiteside Limited
150 Lesmill Road, Don Mills, Ontario

MEXICO AND CENTRAL AMERICA: HARLA S.A. de C.V.
Apartado 30–546, Mexico 4, D. F.

EUROPE: Boxerbooks Inc.
Limmatstrasse 111, 8031 Zurich

THAILAND: Central Department Store Ltd.
306 Silom Road, Bangkok

HONG KONG & SINGAPORE: Books for Asia Ltd.
30 Tat Chee Avenue, Kowloon; 65 Crescent Road, Singapore 15

THE FAR EAST: Japan Publications Trading Company
P.O. Box 5030, Tokyo International, Tokyo

Published by Kodansha International Ltd., 2–12–21 Otowa, Bun-kyo-ku, Tokyo 112 and Kodansha International/USA, Ltd., 10 East 53rd Street, New York, New York 10022 and 44 Montgomery Street, San Francisco, California 94104.
Printed in Japan.

LCC 74-24785
ISBN 0–87011–240–6
JBC 0023–784683–2361

First edition, 1974

CONTENTS

FOREWORD

Lieutenant Hiroo Onoda was officially declared dead in December, 1959. At the time it was thought that he and his comrade Kinshichi Kozuka had died of wounds sustained five years earlier in a skirmish with Philippine troops. A six-month search organized by the Japanese Ministry of Health and Welfare in early 1959 had uncovered no trace of the two men.

Then, in 1972 Onoda and Kozuka surfaced, and Kozuka was killed in an encounter with Philippine police. In the following half year, three Japanese search parties attempted to persuade Onoda to come out of the jungle, but the only response they received was a thank-you note for some gifts they left. This at least established that he was alive. Owing partly to his reluctance to appear, he became something of a legend in Japan.

In early 1974, an amiable Japanese university dropout named Suzuki, who had tramped his way through some fifty countries contributing to the woes of numerous Japanese embassies, took it upon himself to make a journey through the Philippines, Malaysia, Singapore, Burma, Nepal and other countries that might occur to him en route. When he left Japan, he told his friends that he was going to look for Lieutenant Onoda, a panda and the Abominable Snowman, in that order. Presumably the panda and the Snowman are still waiting, because after only four days on Lubang, Suzuki found Onoda and persuaded him to meet with a delegation from Japan, which Suzuki undertook to summon.

7

Reports of Suzuki's meeting with Onoda touched off some of the most extravagant news coverage ever provided by Japanese press and television. People tended for a while to doubt Suzuki, but a mission was quickly dispatched to the Philippines to check on his story. Accompanying the mission were no fewer than one hundred Japanese newsmen.

There are several theories as to why the reappearance of Onoda created such a stir. Mine is that Onoda showed signs of being something that defeat in World War II had deprived Japan of: a genuine war hero. Similar excitement had arisen over earlier returnees. Only a year earlier, Sergeant Shōichi Yokoi had come home from Guam amid great fanfare. Now, however, nobody could conceal the feeling that Yokoi was a rather ordinary man—too ordinary to serve as a hero. Perhaps Lieutenant Onoda would be the real thing.

It became apparent after his surrender that Onoda was intelligent, articulate, strong willed and stoic. This is the way the Japanese like their heroes to be, and in the three weeks between his first contact with Suzuki and his being received by President Ferdinand Marcos, news coverage in Japan swelled to the proportions of a deluge. When Onoda arrived back in Japan, he was received like a triumphant general. Norio Suzuki, for his part, was promoted in one jump from adventurer to assistant hero.

Normally I am almost completely immune to heroes and the adoration thereof. I also tend to be put off by publicity. Mr. Onoda himself was quoted in the newspaper I read as having said he was no hero, and I was prepared to accept that at face value. When they told me his plane would land in Tokyo at four thirty in the afternoon, my reaction was, "Well, what's to prevent it?"

Still, I am human, and when the time arrived, I put my work aside and sat in front of the set like everybody else. And when I saw this small, dignified man emerge from the plane, bow, and then stand rigidly at attention for his ovation, I suddenly realized that he was something I had not seen—a man who was still living in 1944! Or at least only a few days out of it. A man who for the past thirty years must have been carrying around in his head the forgotten wartime propaganda of those times. Odd thoughts ran through my mind. Should I try to meet him, or had somebody else already proved to him that the American devils had no tails? Could he even now be counted upon not to commit harakiri in the palace plaza? How would he react to a Japan that is so radically different, on the surface at least, from what it was in 1944?

In short, I was hooked. With the rest of the nation I was drawn to the box off and on for a couple of weeks, watching Lieutenant Onoda greet his father and friends, Lieutenant Onoda in his hotel, Lieutenant Onoda going to the hospital for his checkup, Lieutenant Onoda having his breakfast, Lieutenant Onoda leaving Tokyo for his hometown in Wakayama Prefecture. I did not even object when the seven o'clock news on the day of his arrival gave Lieutenant Onoda's reunion with his mother top billing over an attempted hijacking then going on over our heads in Tokyo.

It became clear to me that Onoda was no ordinary straggler, but a man of strong determination and principle. Though slight of build, he looks the part of the stern, slightly pompous Japanese army officer of bygone times. I strongly felt that if he had stayed on Lubang for thirty years, he had done so for a definite reason. I wondered what it was, and what the psychology behind it was.

Even as we were all watching the television, Japanese publishers were scrambling for the rights to Onoda's story. He astonished most of them by turning down some of the more handsome offers and choosing a publisher whom he admired because of its youth magazines, which he had enjoyed in prewar times. After meeting and talking with Onoda, it seemed to me that this decision was typical of him, for the sternness that kept him on Lubang is tempered by gentleness and nostalgia for his younger, carefree days. I personally wonder whether it was not this side of his personality that caused him to yield to a happy-go-lucky but obviously sincere Japanese youth, when he had held out against all the others.

Onoda kept neither diary nor journal, but his memory is phenomenal. Within three months of his return, he had dictated two thousand pages of recollections ranging from the most important events to the tiniest details of jungle life. In July, 1974, articles began running in serial form in the weekly *Shūkan Gendai*. Simultaneously preparations were going on for book versions in both Japanese and English, and inquiries were beginning to come in from publishers abroad.

In the course of making the English translation, I had occasion to question Onoda on a number of points, and I was amazed at the vividness with which he could describe what had taken place at a given time or how he had made some article of clothing. He himself made sketches for all of the diagrams and drawings in this book, as well as for many others appearing in a Japanese children's edition.

In preparing the English text, I received much assistance not only from Mr. Onoda himself but from the editorial staff at Kodansha International, who edited my translation with great care and patience.

At the end of his book, Onoda asks himself what he had been fighting for all these years. My opinion is that it was for integrity. Whether Onoda continues to be regarded as a hero is for the future to decide, but I suspect he will, because in the end he won his war.

Charles S. Terry

Tokyo
October 7, 1974

REUNION

I HID IN THE BUSHES, waiting for the time to pass. It was a little before noon on March 9, 1974, and I was on a slope about two hours away from Wakayama Point. My plan was to wait until the time of the evening when it is still just possible to tell one face from another and then approach Wakayama Point rapidly, in a single maneuver. Too much light would mean danger, but if it were too dark, I would not be able to make sure that the person I was meeting was really Major Taniguchi. Also, late twilight would be a good time for making a getaway, if I should have to.

Just after two in the afternoon, I crept cautiously out of my hiding place and crossed the river above the point. Making my way through a grove of palms that ran along the river, I soon came to an area where the islanders cut trees for building.

At the edge of a clearing, I stopped and looked the place over. I could see nobody around. I supposed that the workers must be taking the day off, but to be on the safe side, I camouflaged myself with sticks and dried leaves before dashing across the shelterless area.

I crossed the Agcawayan River and reached a position about three hundred yards from the appointed spot. It was only about four o'clock, so I still had plenty of time. I changed to a camouflage of fresh leaves. There used to be paddy fields at the point, but now it is a grassy plain with a palm tree here and there. Along the river grow bamboo and shrubs.

11

I started up a little hill from which I would be able not only to look down on the point but to keep an eye on the surroundings. This was the place where I had met and talked with Norio Suzuki two weeks before. Just two days earlier a message from Suzuki asking me to meet him here again had been left in the message box we had agreed on, and I had come. I was still afraid it might be a trap. If it was, the enemy might be waiting for me on the hill.

I proceeded with the utmost caution but saw no signs of life. At the top of the hill, I peered out from among the trees and bushes, and on the edge of the point, where Suzuki had put up his mosquito net, I saw a yellow tent. I could make out a Japanese flag waving above it, but I could not see anybody. Were they resting in the tent? Or were they hiding somewhere else waiting for me to show up?

After thirty tense minutes, during which there was no change, I came down the slope and approached a spot only about one hundred yards from the tent. I shifted my position a little to get a different view, but still I saw no one. I decided they must be in the tent and settled down to wait for sunset.

The sun began to sink. I inspected my rifle and retied my boots. I was confident: I could have walked to the tent with my eyes shut, and I felt strong because I had rested while keeping watch. I jumped over a barbed-wire fence and made for the shade of a nearby *bosa* tree, where I paused, took a deep breath, and looked at the tent again. All was still quiet.

The time came. I gripped my rifle, thrust out my chest, and walked forward into the open.

Suzuki was standing with his back to me, between the tent and a fireplace they had rigged up by the riverbank. Slowly he turned around, and when he saw me, he came toward me with arms outstretched.

"It's Onoda!" he shouted. "Major Taniguchi, it's Onoda!"

In the tent, a shadow moved, but I went forward anyway.

Suzuki, eyes bursting with excitement, ran up to me and with both hands clasped my left hand. I stopped about ten yards from the tent, from which there came a voice.

"Is it really you, Onoda? I'll be with you in a minute."

I could tell from the voice that it was Major Taniguchi. Motionless, I waited for him to appear. Suzuki stuck his head in the tent and brought out a camera. From inside, the major, who was shirtless, looked out and said, "I'm changing my clothes. Wait just a minute."

The head disappeared, but in a few moments Major Taniguchi emerged from the tent fully clothed and with an army cap on his head. Taut down to my fingertips, I barked out, "Lieutenant Onoda, Sir, reporting for orders."

"Good for you!" he said, walking up to me and patting me lightly on the left shoulder. "I've brought you these from the Ministry of Health and Welfare."

He handed me a pack of cigarettes with the chrysanthemum crest of the emperor on them. I accepted it and, holding it up before me in proper respect for the emperor, fell back two or three paces. At a little distance, Suzuki was standing ready with his camera.

Major Taniguchi said, "I shall read your orders."

I held my breath as he began to read from a document that he held up formally with both hands. In rather low tones, he read, "Command from Headquarters, Fourteenth Area Army" and then continued more firmly and in a louder voice: "Orders from the Special Squadron, Chief of Staff's Headquarters, Bekabak, September 19, 1900 hours.

"1. In accordance with the Imperial Command, the Fourteenth Area Army has ceased all combat activity.

"2. In accordance with Military Headquarters Command No. A–2003, the Special Squadron in the Chief of Staff's Headquarters is relieved of all military duties.

"3. Units and individuals under the command of the Special

Squadron are to cease military activities and operations immediately and place themselves under the command of the nearest superior officer. When no officer can be found, they are to communicate with the American or Philippine forces and follow their directives.

"Special Squadron, Chief of Staff's Headquarters, Fourteenth Area Army, Major Yoshimi Taniguchi."

After reading this, Major Taniguchi paused slightly, then added, "That is all."

I stood quite still, waiting for what was to follow. I felt sure Major Taniguchi would come up to me and whisper, "That was so much talk. I will tell you your real orders later." After all, Suzuki was present, and the major could not talk to me confidentially in front of him.

I watched the major closely. He merely looked back rather stiffly. Seconds passed, but still he said no more. The pack on my back suddenly seemed very heavy.

Major Taniguchi slowly folded up the order, and for the first time I realized that no subterfuge was involved. This was no trick—everything I had heard was real. There was no secret message.

The pack became still heavier.

We really lost the war! How could they have been so sloppy?

Suddenly everything went black. A storm raged inside me. I felt like a fool for having been so tense and cautious on the way here. Worse that that, what had I been doing for all these years?

Gradually the storm subsided, and for the first time I really understood: my thirty years as a guerrilla fighter for the Japanese army were abruptly finished. This was the end.

I pulled back the bolt on my rifle and unloaded the bullets.

"It must have been a struggle," said Major Taniguchi. "Relax, take it easy."

I eased off the pack that I always carried with me and laid the gun on top of it. Would I really have no more use for this rifle that I had polished and cared for like a baby all these years? Or Kozuka's rifle, which I had hidden in a crevice in the rocks? Had the war really ended thirty years ago? If it had, what had Shimada and Kozuka died for? If what was happening was true, wouldn't it have been better if I had died with them? I walked slowly after Major Taniguchi into the tent.

That night I did not sleep at all. Once inside the tent, I began giving a report of my reconnaissance and military activity during thirty years on Lubang—a detailed field report. Occasionally Major Taniguchi put in a word or two, but for the most part he listened attentively, nodding now and then in agreement or sympathy.

As coolly as possible I reported one event after another, but as I talked, emotion began to overcome me, and when I got to the parts about Shimada and Kozuka dying, I faltered several times. Major Taniguchi blinked as though holding back tears. The only thing that saved me from breaking down completely was the steady snoring of young Suzuki, who had drunk a good deal of sake before going to sleep on his cot.

Before I started my report, Suzuki had asked the major whether he should tell the other searchers that I had turned up. The major told him not to, because if he reported, we would immediately be besieged by a great crowd of people. Suzuki signaled "no change," and I proceeded to talk to the major until dawn.

Several times he ordered me to go to bed and tell him the rest tomorrow, but although I tried this two or three times, each time I was up again in less than ten minutes. How could I sleep at a time like this? I had to tell him everything then and there.

Finally I reached the end of the story, and the major said, "Now let's get some sleep. It will only be an hour or so before the sun is really up. We have a rough day in front of us, and even an hour will help." He must have been relieved that the search was over, because he was snoring seconds after he lay down.

I was not. After sleeping outdoors where best I could for all these years, I could not get used to the cot. I closed my eyes, but I was more awake than ever. Like it or not, I had to go over in my mind all the events that had brought me to this tent.

COMMANDO TRAINING

I was born in 1922 in the town of Kainan, Wakayama Prefecture. When I was at the Kainan Middle School, I was crazy about Japanese fencing (*kendō*). Although I was not exceptionally good at my studies, I liked going to school, because when classes were over, I could to go the *kendō* gym and practice with my bamboo "sword" until I was worn out.

My specialties were a jumping body attack and a side attack to the body. My teacher, Eizaburō Sasaki, was sixth rank at the time, and he taught me those two techniques thoroughly. Sasaki was a small man but was reputed to be the most skillful *kendō* expert in all of Wakayama Prefecture. I myself was only five feet tall then, the smallest boy in the class, and it was a foregone conclusion that anybody I fought against would make straight for my mask. At just the moment when my opponent, having brandished his sword above my head for a time, started to bring it down on my forehead, I would dodge and thrust at his chest. Sasaki took great pains teaching me this technique.

There was one boy in my class I just could not beat. His name was Kaoru Kobai. Later he went to Waseda University and is now a seventh-rank fencer, but at that time he was just another beginner like me. It burned me up that I could not get the best of him. Just once, I thought, just once before we finish school, I have to outdo him.

Suddenly we were in the fifth and last year of school, and the

final *kendō* practice session was ending. I pulled Kobai aside and
said, "Look, I just can't graduate without beating you once.
Give me one more chance. Please!"

He consented to take me on as many times as I wanted, and
we put on our protective gear again. When we faced each
other, everybody else gathered around to watch the match.
I told myself over and over that I mustn't lose, couldn't lose,
and when he started for my mask, as I knew he would, I
lunged forward and to the right. Kobai's breastplate clanged,
and the tip of my sword told me I had struck home.

Afterward Kobai said offhandedly, "That was some thrust,
Onoda," and I, who had been proud only of my technique,
realized that I had not begun to understand the spirit of *kendō*.
I turned red all over.

That year was 1939. In the spring I went to work for a local
trading company named Tajima Yōkō, which specialized in
lacquerware. I took the job on the understanding that I would
be sent to their branch in Hankow (now Wuhan) in central
China. I was seventeen and did not want to live off my parents
any longer. It seemed to me that the time had come to go out
on my own. China was so big that there were bound to be
plenty of opportunities there. I would work hard; I would get
rich. Hankow was a good place to start, because my second
oldest brother, Tadao, who was a first lieutenant in the army,
was stationed there, and he would help me.

I was the fifth of seven children, five boys and two girls.
My oldest brother, Toshio, had gone through the difficult
First High School in Tokyo and the Medical Department of
Tokyo Imperial University. He was now a medical officer in
the army, stationed near the border between Korea and
Manchukuo. The next oldest son was Tadao, and then there
was Chie, my older sister. There had been a third son named
Yoshio, but he died in childhood. Two years younger than I
was the fifth son, Shigeo, who was in the fourth year of middle

school. The youngest was my other sister, Keiko, who was only ten at the time.

I arrived in Hankow about the middle of April and went the same day to see my brother at the officers' quarters. I had not warned him I was coming, and he was dumbfounded. When he recovered, he asked "What's going on? What are you doing here?"

I explained myself. Immediately he gave me to understand that I was not to count on him to look after me.

"Don't you realize you might get killed in China?" he asked.

I pulled myself up and answered, quite loudly, "If a man is not prepared to take a few risks, he will get nowhere!" My brother stared at me, no doubt in disbelief.

He had occasion to stare at me again shortly thereafter. I had left Japan with one suitcase, and it seemed to me that the first thing I should do was to get some good clothes to wear. I decided to ask my brother to buy me a suit; to my surprise he consented. I promptly chose a very good English woolen material and asked the tailor to make me a suit in the London fashion. When my brother received the bill, his eyes nearly popped. It had not occurred to him that a boy of seventeen would even think of spending that much money.

The Hankow branch of Tajima Yōkō was located on a busy downtown street. The showroom was on the first floor, the offices were on the second, and the third floor was a dormitory, where all four members of the staff slept, including the head of the branch. My first job was to keep the branch accounts.

After about a year of working in the office, I was made a buyer and sent around each day to the nearby towns to call on suppliers. The head of the branch was afraid I was too young to be taken seriously, so to bolster my dignity, he bought me a 1936 Studebaker. When I set forth in this splendid vehicle, I thought I was about the greatest businessman in the world.

After the first year, I discovered the dance hall in the French Concession, where, from then on, I danced through the night almost every night. I loved it. Sometimes when I was dancing it seemed hard to believe that only a year ago I had been getting my kicks swinging a bamboo sword in the *kendō* gym.

It was a decidedly fancy dance hall, and it cost a good deal of money for me to go as often as I did. I resolved to ask my brother to pay half of my monthly expenses; for some reason he agreed to do so. As I look back on it, I see that although I needed the money, what I wanted more than that was to be spoiled by my brother. My upbringing had been very strict, and I was starving for affection and indulgence.

One evening when I was dancing, my brother suddenly appeared, in uniform, at the dance hall. Though somewhat flustered, I managed to grab the initiative by telling him to find a partner and join in the fun. He glowered like a demon, but all he said was, "How can I dance dressed like this?" Luckily he made no move to cut off my allowance.

Although I drank little, I smoked about twenty cigarettes a day, and when I played mahjong all night long, as I sometimes did, I smoked fifty or more. I did not have much to do with the other Japanese in Hankow, and for that reason I was soon able to speak Chinese pretty well. My countrymen all said that I was studying up on Chinese to make time with the Chinese girls. This was not entirely untrue, but I was always bashful around girls. My Chinese rarely helped much when I was talking to them.

In January, 1941, when my brother was transferred to the Army Accounting School in Tokyo, I was left to fend for myself. To shore up my self-confidence, I worked harder—and played harder at the dance hall. I knew there were only two more years before I would be drafted. In Hankow I had grown two or three inches taller, and since I had no ailments, I was sure I would be put in Class A when the time came. I wanted to make the most of my two years, for I was conscious that they were all the youth I had left. I was determined to do the best I could at my job and at the same time to have as much fun as possible at that splendid dance hall. If I was lucky, I thought, maybe the war would end; then I would be able to make a lot of money in business. I dreamed of having my own company in China, and to some extent I regarded the evenings at the dance hall as an investment in the future, albeit one that had been financed to a considerable extent by my brother.

On the eighth of December in that year, the war between Japan and the United States began. After that the dance hall and just about everything else had to close shop on the eighth day of each month as a "contribution to the Asian war effort." The Japanese newspapers in Hankow began to call those of us who frequented the French Concession the "vermin of Asia," and anyone who was in the concession until very late at night ran the risk of being picked up by the Japanese military police.

Deprived to a large extent of my greatest pleasure, I decided to learn how to sing, and I started taking voice lessons. Some of the boys in the band at the dance hall had previously offered to give me music lessons in the daytime, but I did not think my fingers would ever be agile enough to play the trumpet or the clarinet. Singing seemed the right answer. I practiced mostly the blues and tangos, sometimes sitting up all night listening to records on the electric Victrola I had installed in my closet.

One day in May, 1942, I was called up for my army physical, which I passed immediately. That evening I cabled my family in Wakayama: "Class A Banzai!" Shortly afterward I was notified that on December 10 I would be inducted into the Sixty-first Infantry Regiment in Wakayama.

Thinking that I ought to get myself into the best possible physical shape, I quit my job with Tajima Yōkō in August and returned to Wakayama. Once at home, I spent my days swimming in the nearby ocean and my evenings practicing *kendō* in the gym at the local police headquarters. I had not practiced for a long time, but I was already second rank when I left middle school, and Mr. Sasaki, my teacher, urged me to try for a higher rank, which he felt would come in handy in the army. Not having worked at the sport for so long, I was a little nervous about the test for third rank, but I passed it. Even after that I continued to work out at the gym every other day until I was inducted.

When I went into the army, I promised my mother I would come back a private first class. Although I had some military courses in middle school and was eligible to take entrance examinations for officers' training school, I did not think I I was cut out to be an officer, nor did I want to wear a uniform different from the others and stand up in front of people barking out orders. The two stars of a private first class were enough for me. At least I thought so at that time.

Ten days after I was inducted, I was assigned to the Two Hundred Eighteenth Infantry Regiment, along with other new inductees from my area. There was a celebration to mark our departure, and then we left. We had no idea where we were being sent, but the noncom in charge of our group passed the word to me that it was Nan-ch'ang. I could hardly believe this, because Nan-ch'ang was where Tadao was now stationed. Any misgivings that I might have had left me when I found that I would be seeing my affluent brother again.

Shortly after the beginning of the year we arrived in Nan-ch'ang, where it was so cold that the rice in my mess kit froze. The minute we got off the train I started shivering all over.

The officers from the base had come to the station to meet us, and we marched by them in four ranks. Out of the corner of my eye I looked for Tadao; presently I spotted him standing a little away from the other officers and wearing a cloak over his overcoat. When we passed him, I stole a quick glance in his direction. He saw me; it was clear from the expression on his face that he was even more surprised than he had been at Hankow. He later told me that his second thought was, "This is going to cost money."

Our squad leader could administer a mean slap when he was angry, but most of the time he was laughing and in good spirits. He called me to him one day and told me that he had chosen me for his squad because he thought I would make a good soldier. He added that I had better make a good soldier.

Our regiment had a reputation for having good legs, and we were constantly being ordered to march three and a half miles in an hour. Sometimes it was five miles, and when that happened, most of the recruits were resentful. Fortunately, my training in *kendō* had prepared me for this, and never once did I break ranks.

I had kept on growing; now I stood five foot four. When I had my physical after basic training, my weight had increased to 132 pounds. which was twice the weight of the full pack we had to carry. I was considered to be just the right size, because anyone who did not weigh twice as much as the pack could not stand up under it in the long haul, and anyone who weighed much more was carrying around excess poundage.

I first came under real fire just after I finished basic training. It was in a place called An-i, which is between Nan-ch'ang and Chiu-chiang, and we were assigned to clean out a troop of enemy guerrillas who had been causing trouble in the area. Our battalion worked out a plan whereby the guerrilla leader was captured alive. But during the operation I injured my right foot and was laid up for a few days, which was particularly unfortunate because it prevented me from taking an examination for officers' training school.

Having said earlier that I wanted nothing grander than the rank of private first class, I must confess that after I went into the army, I changed my mind rather quickly. One reason was that I wanted to do something that would make the squad leader happy. The other was the idea that if I was going to go to war, I might just as well go in one of those flashy officer's uniforms. The attire of a private first class is not inspiring.

I was dejected at having missed the examination, and I suppose I looked glum when I went on my next day off to see my brother. When I told him the trouble, he directed me to stay put and immediately took off on his horse to see the commander of my unit. When the latter found out I was Tadao's brother, he agreed to give me a special examination. I passed it, and on August 1, I was transferred to a preliminary officers' training unit.

Here the men who passed the course were divided into two groups: some went on to more advanced officers' training, while the others remained noncoms. Fortunately, I came out in the first group. Since the regimental commander was in favor of more and better training for officers, he directed that the twelve successful candidates, myself included, be given extra training by Lieutenant Tsunenori Ōno, the regiment's standard-bearer.

Instead of going back to my company, I stayed with the training unit and was given two weeks of training each in machine guns and horsemanship. After that, I had another week of drill in firing the regimental artillery, and I ended up returning to my company for only one night. In the meantime, my brother was transferred from Nan-ch'ang to a new division being formed in Korea.

As a rule, officer candidates who were in China were sent to the Reserve Officers' Training School in Nanking, but in this year they were being sent back to Japan. My group was assigned to a school in Kurume, a port in Kyushu, where we arrived on January 13, 1944.

"The Devil's Kurume," as it was known among the students, was a very tough training camp, and the officer in charge of my class, Captain Shigeo Shigetomi, was considered to be one of the toughest officers there. His motto was "Better to sweat on the training ground than to bleed on the battleground," and he drilled his fifty soldiers constantly in suicide-attack maneuvers. Shigetomi's favorite expressions were, "You're stupid" and "You've got everything backward." These were usually bleated out to the accompaniment of a sharp slap on the misdoer's face.

I learned from Captain Shigetomi what military training was and what it meant to be a soldier. He also taught me spiritual discipline. Soldiers, I was told, are always goofing off or making excuses, but such conduct is not permissible for officers. In our school, the worst disgrace was to be caught unprepared or uninformed. Nothing should be handled in slipshod fashion, no matter how trivial it might seem. Captain Shigetomi made me into an officer, and it was my pride as an officer that sustained me during my thirty years on Lubang.

On March 5, 1944, when I was out on maneuvers, a message came telling me to return to the base on the double to see a visitor. I ran all the way back; the visitor turned out to be Tadao. When he saw me, he said, "What happened to you?"

"Why?" I asked.

"You look like a real man now," came the reply.

My brother had been attached for temporary duty to a division command in Korea and had been in Pyongyang for a while, but as of March 1, he had been ordered to Twenty-third Army Headquarters in Kwangtung. He was to take a plane from Hakata in a day or two, but he had found time to come to see me. We talked for a while, then just as he started to leave, he looked me straight in the eye and said, "Be strong! It won't be long before you're going to need all the strength you have."

I said firmly, "Don't worry, I'll die like a man."

"Well," said my brother, "there is no point in rushing off to get killed. But you'd better be prepared to die in case your turn comes."

I walked with Tadao to the front gate, and just before we got there, he turned to me and asked in a low voice, "Have you ever had a woman?"

I just smiled at him without answering. Our eyes met, and he said heartily, "Well, this is it. Take care of yourself!"

He started to walk away, but at just that point I mustered up the courage to say, "Give me fifty yen to remember you by."

I suppose he had been expecting a touch, because he good-naturedly took out his wallet and started riffling through it. Grumbling that he had no small money, he handed me a hundred-yen note and said with a grin, "I don't suppose it would do any good to ask for my change."

I thought to myself that this was probably our last good-bye. Once more he told me to take care of myself, and then he marched off with great strides, his spit-polished boots glistening in the sun.

In August I finished officers' training and became an apprentice officer. I would have to remain in this status another four months before my commission as a second lieutenant became official. The usual procedure was for apprentice officers to go back to their former units. As it happened, the war situation in the Pacific was so serious by this time that half of the men who had come from China were to be reassigned to units of the Western Army in Kyushu. Since I was not included in that group, I was looking forward to going back to China. I was joking with the others about how great it would be to be filling up on that wonderful Chinese food again when suddenly I was called to headquarters.

There the message was, "You are hereby ordered to the Thirty-third Squadron in the Eastern Sector." This was a unit I had never heard of, so I asked the officer, "What does the squadron do?"

"I can't tell you."

"Where is it stationed?"

"At a place called Futamata, north of Hamamatsu."

That was all I could get out of him, but I could tell I was going to some sort of special unit.

After our graduation ceremony on August 13, some of us went to say good-bye to Captain Shigetomi, who told us all, for the last time, to be good officers. He was almost tearful as he patted each of us on the back and wished us well.

When I arrived at Futamata on August 16, I was told that training would not begin until September 1. I was directed to take a two-week leave in the meantime.

I went to Tokyo, partly because I wanted to get a company officer's sword belt from my oldest brother, who had been promoted to the rank of major and was now entitled to wear a field officer's sword belt. My brother had been transferred to the Army Medical Administration in Tokyo and was living in Nakano, which was then on the outskirts of the city. He asked me about the outfit I was being assigned to; I told him the name of the squadron, adding that I had no idea what it did.

My brother looked startled. "It's this," he said. He first

stuck out the index and middle fingers of his right hand and then made a motion like that of pouring water into a teapot. I assumed he was being secretive because his wife was present. I merely nodded my understanding.

Not that I understood completely. The pointed fingers meant a karate thrust into an opponent's eyes, and the gesture of pouring tea suggested giving someone a dose—of poison. I took this to mean that I was to be engaged in some sort of spying, but I was not sure what sort. The idea that I might be assigned to intelligence work was not particularly surprising to me, because back in Nan-ch'ang Lieutenant Ōno had once said to me, "We are short of good people for the pacification squads. With your Chinese, when you finish officers' training school, you ought to be given a job in that field."

"Pacification squad" was the current term for units that infiltrated behind enemy lines and tried to break down defenses from within. They corresponded in many ways to what the Americans called "commando squadrons."

The next day my brother gave me the sword belt, and after I had gone to pay my respects before the imperial palace, Yasukuni Shrine and Meiji Shrine, I went to Wakayama to see the rest of my family.

The training center I went to was properly called the Futamata Branch of the Nakano Military School, but the sign over the gate said only Futamata Army Training Squadron. It was no more than a small collection of decrepit army barracks, located a little more than a mile from Futamata railway station. The school was not far from a place on the Tenryū River that had once been used by the Third Engineer Corps from Nagoya as a practice area for army bridge builders.

My group was the branch school's first class, and on September 1 there was an opening ceremony. The commandant,

Lieutenant Colonel Mamoru Kumagawa, addressed our class of 230 officers with words to the following effect: "The purpose of this branch school is to train you in secret warfare. For that reason, the real name of the school is to be kept absolutely secret. Furthermore, you yourselves are to discard any ideas you may have had of achieving military honors."

This came as no shock to me, because my brother had warned me in Tokyo, but the others looked at each other in amazement and anxiety. The anxiety only increased when one of the instructors, Lieutenant Sawayama, stood up and started shooting questions at us.

"When you gentlemen arrived in Futamata, what impression did it make on you?" he asked. Then, without waiting for answers:

"If there were troops stationed here, how many battalions do you think there would be?

"What is the principal industry here?

"Just what kind of a town is this?

"How much food do you think the town could provide for army troops?

"What is the average frontage of the houses here?"

Of course none of us had the foggiest idea of the answers. We were stupefied!

Then he continued, "I am trying to show you what we mean by the word *intelligence*. To make the maps necessary for military movements, we must have information—intelligence, that is—from many different quarters. My job is to teach you how to acquire intelligence as it relates to military needs. You will have to learn to notice everything around you and evaluate it from the viewpoint of military intelligence."

I had foreseen something like this, but I could not suppress the feeling that I had wandered into a rat's nest. I was not the only one by far.

Somebody said, "I don't have enough brains for this."

Another moaned, "Does this mean that on top of officers' training I have to become a spy?"

That evening several of them went to see Lieutenant Sawayama, and their spokesman told him, "We have all thought since we came into the army that one day we would lead a platoon into battle. That's why we worked so hard at officers' training school. And what we learned there was how to be effective leaders in battle. We don't know anything about secret warfare, and we are not at all sure of our ability to learn. We would like to be returned to our former units."

The next morning Lieutenant Sawayama called us together and addressed us: "You're quite right in thinking that the training here will be difficult, but the very fact that you understand this merely on the basis of what I said yesterday shows that you have good minds. I intend to cram into your heads eveything you need to know, so don't worry. And don't come to me a second time with your bellyaching!"

I, for one, was at least happy to be told that I had a good brain. I cannot say that all my fears had been dispelled, but I made up my mind to try to learn everything there was to learn at Futamata.

It was certainly different from the officers' training school. Military forms and procedures were observed, but without excessive emphasis on regulations. On the contrary, the instructors kept stressing to us that in our new role as commando trainees, we should learn that so long as we kept the military spirit and remained determined to serve our country, the regulations were of little importance. At the same time, they tried to impress upon us that the more underhanded techniques that we were learning, such as wiretapping, were to be used against the enemy, not for our own personal benefit. They urged us to express our opinions concerning the quality of the instruction and to make complaints if we felt like it.

We had four hours of training in the morning and four in

the afternoon. Classes lasted two hours each, with fifteen-minute breaks in midmorning and midafternoon. When the time for a break came, everybody piled out of the classroom windows into the yard to have a smoke. There were 230 of us, packed like sardines into one small barracks, and the break was not long enough for all of us to leave and return in orderly fashion via the door. At officers' training school if anyone had dared leave by the window, the punishment would have been swift and severe. At Futamata it was routine.

The classroom was terribly cramped. We were not only literally shoulder to shoulder but almost completely pinned in front and back by desks. The instructor lectured from a tiny platform, occasionally squeezing his way into one of the few narrow aisles. Despite the uncomfortable conditions, the lecturers displayed much enthusiasm, even fervor, in propounding the essentials of guerrilla warfare.

At the main school in Nakano, the course had at first consisted of one year of language training and one year of guerrilla and ideological training. As the war situation grew more serious, the language training was eliminated, and the remainder of the course was reduced to six months. By the time we came along, the six-month course was being jammed into three months. The pace was fierce for both instructors and trainees.

I began to understand the basic differences between open warfare and secret warfare. The attack drills at the officers' training school had been lessons in open warfare, which is fundamentally unicellular. We were now being taught a multi-cellular type of warfare in which every available particle of information is used to throw the enemy into confusion. In one sense, what we were learning at Futamata was the exact opposite of what we had been taught before. We had to accustom ourselves to a whole new concept of war.

And the homework was mountainous! Almost every night

we had to request permission to leave the lights on after hours, and most of us were up until midnight regularly. Even so, there was not enough time. On our days off we would hole up in the inns in Futamata to work on our assignments. I always stayed at one of two inns, the Kadoya or the Iwataya, and recently I was interested to find that the Kadoya is still operating today. It must have been a terrible nuisance for the innkeepers to have this horde of fledgling officers descend on them every Sunday, particularly when there was a shortage of food.

I cannot think of Futamata without being reminded of the famous folk song "Sado Okesa." Lieutenant Sawayama used this song to illustrate the whole idea of secret warfare.

"There is," he said, "no correct version of 'Sado Okesa.' Within certain broad limits, you can sing it or dance it any way you like. And people do just that. The type of guerrilla warfare that we teach at this school is the same. There are no fixed rules. You do what seems best suited to the time and the circumstances."

In one sense, the training we received can be compared with what is usually called "liberal education." We were to a large degree given our heads, so to speak. We were encouraged to think for ourselves, to make decisions where no rules existed. Here again the training was very different from what we had experienced at the officers' training school. There we were taught not to think but to lead our troops into battle, resolved to die if necessary. The sole aim was to attack enemy troops and slaughter as many as possible before being slaughtered. At Futamata, however, we learned that the aim was to stay alive and continue to fight as guerrillas as long as possible, even if this entailed conduct normally considered disgraceful. The question of how to stay alive was to be decided at one's own discretion.

I liked this. This kind of training and this kind of warfare seemed to suit my personality.

At that time, if a soldier who had been taken prisoner later managed to return to Japan, he was subject to a court martial and a possible death penalty. Even if the penalty was not carried out, he was so thoroughly ostracized by others that he might as well have been dead. Soldiers were supposed to give their lives for the cause, not grovel in enemy prison camps. General Hideki Tōjō's *Instructions for the Military* said explicitly: "He who would not disgrace himself must be strong. He must remember always the honor of his family and his community, and he must strive fervently to live up to their trust in him. Do not live in shame as a prisoner. Die, and leave no ignominious crime behind you!"

But at Futamata, we were taught that it was permissible to be taken prisoner. By becoming prisoners, we were told, we would place ourselves in a position to give the enemy false information. Indeed, there might be times when we ought deliberately to let ourselves be captured. This could, for instance, be the best course when there was a need to communicate directly with others who had already been taken prisoner. In short, the lesson was that the end justifies the means.

In such circumstances, we learned, we would not be held liable by the army for having been captured. Instead we would gain merit for having carried out our duty properly. Only insiders, however, would ever know that we had been engaged in secret warfare, and we would have to face the taunts of outsiders as best we could. Practically no one would be aware of our service to our country, but that is the fate of those engaged in secret warfare. It is not rewarding work, in the ordinary sense of the term.

In what, then, can those engaged in this kind of warfare place their hope? The Nakano Military School answered this question with a simple sentence: "In secret warfare, there is integrity."

And this is right, for integrity is the greatest necessity when a man must deceive not only his enemies but his friends. With integrity—and I include in this sincerity, loyalty, devotion to duty and a sense of morality—one can withstand all hardships and ultimately turn hardship itself into victory. This was the lesson that the instructors at Futamata were constantly trying to instill in us.

One of them put it this way: "If you are genuinely pure in spirit, people will respond to you and cooperate with you." This meant to me that so long as I remained pure inside, whatever measures I saw fit to take would eventually redound to the good of my country and my countrymen.

At this time we already knew that research on the atomic bomb was being carried on in the United States. It was being carried on in Japan, too, but the reports we received indicated that America, which had far greater wealth and far more scientists, was considerably ahead of Japan. Although our reports were little better than rumors, we foresaw that eventually an atomic weapon would be used against Japan.

In October, 1944, the American forces landed on Leyte, and the overall situation was so grim that people were beginning to talk seriously of an invasion of the homeland. We felt that every minute was bringing us closer to the time when we would be called into action. And yet we were not seriously disturbed. We were sure that even if the enemy did land in Japan, in the end Japan would win. Like nearly all of our countrymen, we considered Japan to be the invincible land of the gods.

In early November, we carried out a graduation maneuver to show how well we had learned our lessons. The problem was posed to us as follows: "An enemy force has landed in Japan.

Enemy troops have occupied the airfield at Hamamatsu. As fighting progresses, the enemy commander is preparing to fly from Hamamatsu to Atsugi Air Base. You are to move into action immediately. Your mission is to kidnap the enemy commander and blow up the Hamamatsu airfield."

Each of us had to draw up a plan for carrying out the mission. The best plan was then selected, and the manueuver was put into simulated operation.

Since I was assigned to the kidnap group, I wore my uniform, minus insignia. The demolition team dressed up as farmers and day laborers. An advance lookout was dispatched, but as he crept toward the airfield, he sighted an "enemy" force approaching. He hastily dived into a side road, but by this time his movements had aroused the suspicion of farmers working in the nearby fields, who then closed in on him. Instead of making a futile attempt to escape, he gave himself up to the "enemy." Later he told me, "I saw there was no use resisting, so I decided to get caught and then grudgingly give the enemy a lot of false dope." It struck me that he had learned the "Sado Okesa" lesson well.

Other than the capture of the lookout, the maneuver, which lasted four days and three nights, went off without a hitch. Observers from Army General Headquarters gave us high marks. Not long after that, I heard that while the maneuver was going on, a rumor spread among the people in the neighborhood that an army officer in Futamata named Kumagawa had organized a rebellion and was about to send a task force of officer trainees to blow up the airfield. Some of the local people thought the military police should be notified immediately, but others urged caution, and the decision was put off until the following morning. By that time the maneuver had ended, and nothing more came of the affair.

On November 30, our class received orders to "withdraw" from the school. I still do not know why, when we had completed our course, we were ordered to "withdraw," rather than given some recognition of our graduation, but in any event I was confident that those three months had done wonders for my spirit, as well as for my capability as a soldier. I felt that I would be able to conduct myself as cleverly and as coolly as the captured lookout who had been my fellow trainee. I told myself that whatever happened, I would be able to carry out my duties creditably.

Just before we finished school, word was received that forty-three of the trainees, including myself, would be sent to the Philippines, and twenty-two of us were directed to reassemble at Futamata on December 7.

On the evening before I left to go on leave, I walked down to the banks of the Tenryū River and stared for a time at the rushing waters. Suddenly I remembered a popular song called "Kantarō of Ina," which was going around at the time. The words went:

> I may look like a crook and a ruffian.
> But witness, O Moon, the splendor of my heart.

The inspiration for this was a historical tale about a gangster named Kantarō, who had aided the emperor's troops during the Meiji Restoration. Standing here by the river I saw the secret warfare troops, of whom I was one, as gangsters like Kantarō, stealthily providing aid for the valiant imperial troops in the field.

I came to the conclusion then that I would probably go off to the Philippines and carry on my guerrilla warfare in the mountains until I died there all alone, lamented by no one. Although I knew that my struggle would bring me neither fame nor honor, I did not care.

I asked myself, "Is this the way it ought to be?"

And I answered, "This is the way it ought to be. If it is of the slightest use to my country, I shall be happy."

As I went on with the song, my voice rose above the sound of the turbulent river:

O Moon of my homeland, I am newly reborn.
Mirror the brightness of my soul tonight.

I went home to Wakayama for the first time in three months. This would be my last visit for a long time, perhaps forever, and I said to my mother, "Let me have that dagger you keep in the drawer of your cabinet."

The dagger was a last-resort weapon that had been handed down from my great-grandmother to my grandmother and then to my mother. I remembered hearing my mother tell how her mother had given it to her when she married my father. It was in a white scabbard, and as she handed it to me, she said gravely, "If you are taken captive, use this to kill yourself."

I nodded, but inside I knew that I was not going to commit suicide even if I were taken captive. To do so would be a violation of my duty as a secret warfare agent. I coaxed the dagger from her simply because I wanted it for self-protection.

I also wanted something to remember my father by, but I could not bring myself to ask him. While I was trying to decide what to do, I thought of a bamboo incense tube of which he was very fond. It was about a foot long, with a black sandalwood stopper and a beautiful inscription carved on the side. My father always kept it beside a metal incense burner on a small three-drawer cabinet in the living room. I made up my mind just to swipe it. When I told my mother what I was going to do, she did not object.

Later, my two brothers told me that when they heard I had taken the dagger and the incense tube, they were shocked. They thought I was thinking of lighting the incense and committing ceremonial harakiri in front of it. Nothing could have been farther from my mind, of course. I just thought that some day when I was at the front, it might be comforting to burn some incense from the tube and think of home.

When I left Wakayama, I told my mother, "My work being what it is, it's possible that I may be reported dead when I'm not. If you're told I've been killed, don't think too much about it, because I may well show up again after a few years."

The next day I went to see my younger brother, Shigeo, who was stationed at Yachimata, in Chiba Prefecture, east of Tokyo. By this time he had received his commission as a second lieutenant and was in training at an aerial reconnaissance school. He wanted to go up to the port of Choshi for dinner. He said there was a restaurant he often went to there where you could eat all the fresh fish you could hold, and that was unusual in those days of shortages. Unfortunately, I did not have time, so we ended by having a farewell meal in a restaurant in Chiba City, which was on my way back to Tokyo.

The next morning my oldest brother saw me off at Tokyo Station.

"Take care of yourself," he said.

FATEFUL ORDERS

The day after I returned to Futamata, there was a strong earthquake. The group of twenty-two to which I belonged had received orders to proceed to Utsunomiya airfield, sixty miles or so north of Tokyo, and board a transport plane that evening. Normally, we would have gone on the Tokaido Railway Line as far as Tokyo. Because of the earthquake, traffic on this line was interrupted, so we had to start out by truck, hoping that the trains would be running farther to the north.

When the truck passed the Kadoya, the inn where I had often stayed, the proprietor and his whole family were waiting outside to say good-bye. We stopped, and they handed us a bottle of sake and a tray loaded with parched chestnuts and dried squid. Without getting off the truck, we broke open the bottle and exchanged farewell toasts.

We managed to catch a train in Kakegawa, then changed trains in Tokyo, arriving at Utsunomiya in the middle of the night. It turned out that the transport plane was undergoing repairs, and we had to kill a few days at an inn in front of Utsunomiya Station. During that interval, we received news that American forces had landed at San Jose on the island of Mindoro in the Philippines. Hearing this, we looked at each other in apprehension, and I felt my body tense.

The twenty-two of us left Utsunomiya airfield on three airplanes, a No. 97 Converted Heavy Bomber-Transport and two

39

No. 100 Heavy Bombers. This was on December 17, two days after San Jose fell. The plan was to fly in one hop to Taipei, refuel, and continue on to Clark Airbase on Luzon the same day, but we were forced down in Okinawa by bad weather and had to stay there three days. Then it developed that the transport required more repairs; with one thing and another, we did not arrive at Clark until December 22, six whole days after leaving Utsunomiya.

When we landed, an air raid warning was in effect, but I was surprised to see the maintenance crews walking around as though nothing was happening. I asked why, and one of them said, "It's Manila's turn today." The enemy was bombing Clark one day and Manila the next.

We had been told that on arrival we were to make contact with the Special Intelligence Squadron of the Fourteenth Area Army. In fact, when we arrived, Masaru Shimoda and Kusuo Tsuchihashi had been sent from the squadron to wait for us. They left almost immediately to report our arrival to squadron headquarters in Manila, fifty miles away, assuring us that they would be back by morning at the latest.

At noon the next day they were still not back. We were afraid something had happened to them on the way, but a few minutes later they drove up in a truck. They explained that a P–38 Lockheed Lightning had spotted them and given chase, forcing them to dodge in and out of side roads most of the way. The strain and excitement of running for their lives still showed on their faces.

We stayed one more night at Clark and then went to Manila on the twenty-fourth. That morning a low-flying enemy Consolidated B–24 had dropped Christmas cards on the city. Addressed to the Philippine people, they bore a picture of a lamb and a message in English saying: "We are now in the South Pacific, hoping to ring in a Happy New Year with you!" When one of my fellow officers translated this for me, I gritted my teeth and said, "Fools! Idiots! Who do they think they are!"

The Special Intelligence Squadron was located in what had been a foreign residential district in Manila. It was in a two-story concrete building, and the sign over the entrance said "Institute of Natural Science."

We were greeted by a darkish man who turned out to be Major Yoshimi Taniguchi, the squadron commander. After we had presented our credentials, the major told me that I, together with five others, would be stationed with the Sugi Brigade, as the Eighth Division from Hirosaki was known. Future orders, he said, would come from division headquarters.

The Sugi Brigade was in charge of defending the west central part of Luzon from Nasugbu to Batangas. Its headquarters were in Lipa.

That night we held a farewell gathering in the "institute." Those of us from Futamata realized that we were perhaps splitting up for the last time, but we had been expecting this. I saw no signs of gloom, though the party was quiet. We drank cold sake with each other, and Major Taniguchi filled us in on the war situation. I was not particularly moved.

On December 26, in the middle of the night, the six of us who were going to the Sugi Brigade left Manila with Major Taniguchi in a truck that was also carrying a fairly large load of ammunition. Dressed in summer uniforms, with swords, revolvers and binoculars, the six of us looked like ordinary army officers, but Major Taniguchi wore the uniform of the Philippine Area Police and a mountain climber's hat.

Under bright moonlight, the truck made its way south toward Lipa. Not long after we started, I saw Bay Lake over to the left, and the sight of its calm moonlit surface relaxed the tension inside me. It was hard to believe that this beautiful landscape was soon to become a battlefield. The scene was unearthly, enchanting, but I was soon brought back to reality by the noise of the transport trucks that passed going the other way. As we went farther south, their number increased.

Our own truck arrived at division headquarters just before dawn. The orders that I was to receive here would decide my fate for the next thirty years.

The road, which had been hurriedly constructed by the Engineer Corps, ran deep into a forest of palms. Sugi Brigade headquarters were located just off to one side of the road. The installation consisted of a scattering of nipa houses, round huts like the ones the natives lived in, with plain boarded walls and roofs thatched with palm leaves. We followed Major Taniguchi into one of them.

Inside were a number of officers: Lieutenant Colonel Motoyama of Strategic Command, Major Takahashi of Intelligence Command, Captain Yamaguchi of the Rear Squadron, First Lieutenant Kusano of the Intelligence Squadron, and a few others.

We waited tensely in a corner of the room while Major Taniguchi and Major Takahashi talked in low voices about how we should be assigned. Sensing that this was a moment of destiny for me, I clenched my fists. After a while, Shigeru Moriguchi and Shigeichi Yamamoto were called over and ordered to lead fifty troops in an attack on San Jose. Next Shin Furuta and Ichirō Takaku were assigned to lead a guerrilla group on the island of Mindoro.

Now it was my turn. Major Takahashi said, "Apprentice Officer Onoda will proceed to Lubang Island, where he will lead the Lubang Garrison in guerrilla warfare."

This was the first time I ever heard of Lubang. I had no idea where it was or how big it was.

Major Takahashi wrote out an order for the Lubang Garrison and affixed to it the seal of the Eighth Division Com-

mander, Lieutenant General Yokoyama. He said, "I'll wire
them orders, but take this along just in case."

The order read: "The commander of the Lubang Garrison
will deploy other squadrons and prepare for guerrilla warfare.
This order does not include groups under senior officers. Apprentice Officer Hiroo Onoda is being sent to lead guerrilla
operations."

After I read this paper, Major Takahashi said, "Our objective is to hamper the enemy attack on Luzon. The first
thing for you to do is destroy the Lubang airfield and the pier
at the harbor. Should the enemy land and try to use the airfield,
destroy their planes and kill the crews."

Major Taniguchi added, "There ought to be at least two
leaders for a guerrilla mission, but we can't spare another man.
You'll have to take care of it by yourself. It won't be easy, but
do the best you can. When you do something by yourself the
first time, you're almost bound to slip up somewhere, so keep
your eyes open."

The only one of the six left was Misao Yamazaki, and when
he had been told that he would stay at division headquarters
as a reserve replacement, the issuing of orders came to an end.
We new arrivals were next supposed to report for duty officially
to the division commander, but as it happened, Lieutenant
General Akira Mutō, Chief of Staff of the Fourteenth Area
Army, had dropped in on division headquarters on his way
back from an inspection tour and was now in the division
commander's room.

General Mutō being the senior officer present, we reported
first to him. Looking us over carefully, he said, "I knew you
were coming, but I thought I'd be too busy to see you. I'm
glad we happened to meet here. The war is not going well at
the moment. It is urgent that you exert every effort to carry
out your orders. Understand? I mean it!"

It was a strange feeling to receive a pep talk from a famous

general. We were honored and impressed. When we started
to report to the division commander, he raised his hand and
stopped us. "Don't worry about me," he said. "You've already
reported to His Excellency the Chief of Staff."

Then, with his eyes directly on me, he said, "You are absolutely forbidden to die by your own hand. It may take three
years, it may take five, but whatever happens, we'll come back
for you. Until then, so long as you have one soldier, you are to
continue to lead him. You may have to live on coconuts. If
that's the case, live on coconuts! Under no circumstances are
you give up your life voluntarily."

A small man with a pleasant face, the commander gave me
this order in a quiet voice. He sounded like a father talking to
a child. When he finished, I responded as briskly as I could,
"*Yes, Sir!*"

I remembered again what I had been taught at Futamata,
and I vowed to myself that I would carry out my orders.
Here I was, only an apprentice officer, receiving my orders
directly from a division commander! That could not happen
very often, and I was doubly impressed with the responsibility
I bore. I said to myself, "I'll do it! Even if I don't have coconuts, even if I have to eat grass and weeds, I'll do it! These
are my orders, and I will carry them out." It may sound
strange today, but I meant it.

Most civilians do not know that in the army orders must
come from a direct superior. The officers who have the authority
to issue orders are the division commander, the regimental
commander and the company commander. Platoon leaders
or detachment leaders are no more than assistants to the company commander, and the orders they issue merely implement
those issued by him.

When a man is standing sentry on his own commander's

orders and an officer from another outfit orders him to do something else, the sentry does not have to obey. He should inform the officer that he is on sentry duty and cannot leave his post until the order comes from his own commander. This is true even if the visiting officer is a general.

At Futamata I was ordered to duty with the Fourteenth Area Army and subsequently assigned to the Sugi Brigade. No company or regimental commander interceded in the issuance of these orders. My direct superior was the commander of the Sugi Brigade, who had ordered me to Lubang. Major Taniguchi and Major Takahashi had the authority to instruct me or direct me, but they had no authority to alter Lieutenant General Yokoyama's orders to me.

It was possible for an officer to have the authority to deploy troops without being able to change orders previously issued to them by their immediate superior. Deployment did not take precedence over orders. When I went to Lubang, I went with orders to *lead* the men in guerrilla warfare but not to *command* them. I could tell them how the thing should be done and make them do it that way, but it was up to their immediate superiors to decide whether they were to engage in guerrilla warfare. In the days that ensued, this lack of authority turned out to be a terrible encumbrance to me.

After reporting for duty and receiving my orders, I went back to the staff room. As I entered, Major Takahashi laughed and said, "Onoda, you'll be surprised at the treat in store for you on Lubang. Why, that oufit there is the best in the whole Japanese army!"

Major Taniguchi, shooting him a reproving look, said, "He's joking."

At this point Squadron Leader Yamaguchi suddenly smiled. "Anyway," he said, "Lubang is a very good island. There aren't many like it anymore. There's always plenty to eat there, Onoda. At least you don't have to worry about that."

Major Taniguchi's face grew more serious as he said, "Those of us who were trained in secret warfare were prepared to have to go behind enemy lines and command foreign troops. You must consider it an honor, Onoda, to be able to lead His Majesty's own men."

"Yes, Sir!" I replied loudly.

He was right. We had indeed been trained to organize and lead foreign troops behind enemy lines. To be put in charge of Japanese soldiers was a privilege. At least they would understand my language.

Major Taniguchi gave me two maps showing Lubang and tried to impress on me the island's strategic importance. "No matter how difficult it may be to carry on your guerrilla campaign," he said, "you must think a very long time before moving on to another island."

One of the maps he gave me was on a scale of 500,000:1. The names on it were written in Japanese, which was a help, but Lubang itself was no bigger than a playing card, and there was almost no information about the terrain. The other map was 25,000:1 and showed all the reefs around the island, but here again it was difficult to tell much about the lay of the land.

"Drop into squadron headquarters on your way to the port, and I'll give you an aerial map they made when the Lubang airfield was built," said Major Taniguchi. With that he collected the two men who were going to Mindoro and left the staff room.

After everybody had gone, I went to the division ordnance depot and procured some necessary equipment—dynamite, land mines, hand grenades and so on—which I had loaded on a truck. I also put a camouflage uniform I had received from the squadron on the truck. That night I spread out the two maps on the floor of the nipa house I was in and examined them by candlelight. Lubang Island was very small. Would it be big enough for guerrilla warfare?

Well, big enough or not, I had my orders and my equipment, and there was nothing to do now but get on with it. I closed my eyes, and once again I heard the division commander's promise: "Whatever happens, we'll come back for you."

I said aloud to myself, "I will fight till that day comes."

On December 30, I received five thousand yen in military currency from Major Takahashi to cover special expenses and then departed from division headquarters. On the truck with me were a sergeant named Suzuki and six of his men, who were going to Lubang to bring back aviation fuel left there. The airplanes had already withdrawn to Luzon, but the fuel and bombs, as well as some of the personnel, were still on Lubang.

When I went to squadron headquarters in Manila, Major Taniguchi had gone to see Yamamoto and the others off, and no one was sure when he would be back. Someone went through the major's desk for me, but could not find the aerial map I had hoped to obtain. I was disappointed, but I decided that after I reached Lubang, I could simply reconnoiter the whole place with my own eyes.

By the side of Banzai Bridge, which they told me was named by General Masaharu Homma, Commander of the Fourteenth Area Army, I found a native motor-sail vessel waiting for me. It was named, in Japanese style, *Seifuku* Maru and must have weighed about fifty tons. The captain, who was about forty, looked over the side and shouted, "Go on and load all your stuff on the boat."

I told him that my cargo consisted of explosives, which he had the right to refuse if he wanted to. Major Takahashi had told me that if he did refuse, a military diesel vessel would be sent to take them.

"I don't mind the explosives," called the captain, "but you'll have to get a permit from Port Headquarters."

I set off to procure the permit, and as I was doing so, the lieutenant in charge asked, "Are you going to leave the explosives on Lubang and come back on the boat?"

"I am not coming back," I answered. "I'm going to Lubang to use the explosives."

The lieutenant stared at me for a moment and said, "Sorry to hear that. Have a beer with me as a farewell drink."

He offered me a bottle of San Miguel, but I thanked him and told him I did not drink. This was not quite true, but I was in a hurry.

"Too bad," he said. "Anyway, I wish you the best of luck."

His genial manner had a calming effect on me. I felt a little ashamed of myself for not accepting his hospitality.

Back at Banzai Bridge, the cargo had already been transferred from the truck to the ship. It had rained, then stopped for a while, and now it was starting again. I sat down cross-legged under a shelter on the deck of the ship with the other soldiers, and we ate the dinner that the crew had prepared for us.

The captain told me that there had been a fair number of private motor-sail craft in Manila doing transport work for the army, but when the enemy landed in Mindoro, they all moved up to Lingayen Gulf. "Mine is the only one left," he said.

I asked why he had not run away with the rest, and he replied, "I need the money. Actually, the way prices are climbing, I can't even get by on the money I receive from the army. That's why I make trips to Lubang. The islanders raise a lot of cows, and every time I go I bring back some to sell in Manila. Division headquarters gave me permission."

He said he had contracted to make five trips to Lubang and this was the third. I recalled a conversation I had had with Lieutenant Yamaguchi.

Norio Suzuki

1. Thirty years of guerrilla warfare in the mountainous jungles of Lubang came to an end on March 9, 1974, when Major Yoshimi Taniguchi read my final orders.

2. On the evening of March 10, 1974, I formally surrendered at the radar base on Lubang Island. Akihisa Kashiwai, the leader of the search party, and I salute, as Major General J. L. Rancudo of the Philippine Air Force inspects my sword.

Philippine Embassy, Tokyo

3–6. *Above left*, at home at the age of ten; *above right*, the *kendō* club at school. The man in kimono is Eizaburō Sasaki, I am on his right, and Kaoru Kobai is at the right end of the back row. *Left*, the Hankow branch of Tajima Yōkō; *below*, a view of Hankow around 1940.

7–10. *Above left*, oldest brother Toshio, his wife and myself in 1942; *above right*, during preliminary officer's training in 1943. *Center*, the Futamata branch of the Nakano Military School. *Below*, an aerial view of Lubang Island from the south.

Keisuke Kumagiri

Hisao Iwanaga

14–17. Defense of the island collapsed in March, 1945, but the last of the Japanese troops, forty-one in number, did not surrender until April, 1946 (*below*). *Above*, Private First Class Yūichi Akatsu (*left*) surrendered in 1949, Corporal Shōichi Shimada (*center*) was killed in 1954, and Private First Class Kinshichi Kozuka (*right*) was killed in 1972.

11–13. Lubang Island lies about seventy-five miles southwest of Manila. Above is the harbor at Tilik and the pier, which I was ordered to blow up. *Center*, looking to the southeast from the town of Ambulong, Snake Mountain is in the center and the mountain we called Six Hundred is to the right. *Below*, the Vigo River.

Keisuke Kumagiri

Asahi Newspaper

Philippine Embassy, Tokyo

18–21. Clothing and equipment were, of course, soon reduced to basic necessities, "requisitioning" from the islanders being the only way to replenish supplies. *Above*, trousers, jacket, cap, leggings and mittens. *Below*, scissors, needles, thread and cloth; backpack; canteen, bowl and buckets.

22–27. *Above*, Using a lens to ignite charcoal was one method of making a fire. Bolo knives were among the items taken from the islanders. *Left*, the dagger I received from my mother, my sword and a model 38 rifle show the effects of the humid climate. *Right*, beef was preserved by drying it over a fire for several nights. Bottles were best for storing ammunition. A tool we made was used for scrapping out coconuts and digging.

Asahi Newspaper

Kodansha

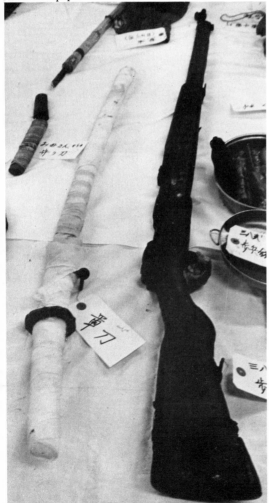

Kodansha

Kodansha

Kyodo News Service

Kodansha

28. Outside the towns, houses like these were built at the foot of mountains.

29. We sometimes killed water buffaloes for food; the islanders use them as beasts of burden.

"The other day," he had said, "when I went to Manila to pick up gasoline, I saw a boat coming from Lubang. There were lots of cows lying on the deck with their legs tied up. You shouldn't have any food problem on Lubang."

That night at nine the *Seifuku* Maru left the harbor at Manila. At first we sailed due west. Although the sea was smooth, it was still raining, and the harbor was pitch-dark.

At one in the morning, we passed the island of Corregidor, in the mouth of the bay. Instead of following the shoreline, we continued to sail west, because enemy torpedo boats were always popping in and out of the offshore waters. It was completely dark; the only sound was the engine. We were moving at a speed of about nine knots. I stood by the captain in the tiny steering compartment and peered out into the darkness. At any moment, an enemy boat might loom up by our side. Indeed, there might at that very instant be a boat out there aiming its guns at us. With all those explosives on board, one hit would have sent us sky high in small bits. I cannot say, however, that I was particularly disturbed. If it was going to happen, it would happen. There was nothing I could do about it.

"If I get killed," I thought, "I'll be enshrined as a god at Yasukuni Shrine, and people will worship me. That isn't so bad."

How many more Japanese soldiers must have been telling themselves the same thing!

The captain shifted the rudder sharply, and the boat tilted slightly as we turned due south. "If we go directly south from here," he said, "we'll land at a harbor called Tilik."

I nodded without saying anything, but my body tensed. Tilik was the name of the port where I had been ordered to blow up the pier.

The rain stopped around dawn. I had not slept all night. The island of Lubang began to appear over the distant horizon.

Gradually it grew larger, and before long I could make out the individual palm leaves through my binoculars. There were mountains, but it looked as though the highest could not be more than fifteen to eighteen hundred feet high. My first impression of Lubang was that it was going to be difficult terrain for guerrilla warfare.

The *Seifuku* Maru picked up speed and approached the island.

NO WILL TO FIGHT

Lubang is a long narrow island, about six miles from north to south and eighteen miles from east to west. When I arrived there, the military force included the Lubang Garrison (a platoon detached from the Three Hundred Fifty-seventh Independent Regiment) under the command of Second Lieutenant Shigenori Hayakawa; the Airfield Garrison under Second Lieutenant Suehiro; a radar squad under Second Lieutenant Tategami (who like me was born in Wakayama); an air intelligence squad under Second Lieutenant Tanaka; and a navy group but no navy officers. The Lubang Garrison had about fifty men, the Airfield Garrison twenty-four, the radar and air intelligence outfits a total of about seventy, and the navy group seven. In addition, there was an air maintenance crew of about fifty-five under Second Lieutenant Ōsaki, who had already received their orders to withdraw but were still there.

It was still not completely light when the *Seifuku* Maru arrived at the pier in Tilik, but the captain ordered the crew to camouflage the ship with palm leaves. The truck that had brought the aviation fuel to the harbor was standing on the pier. I boarded it, along with the captain of the ship and the sergeant responsible for taking the gasoline back to Luzon, and we set off for the town of Lubang, where Lieutenant Suehiro's garrison was stationed.

The town was toward the west end of the island, and the

51

commanders all snapped at me that their troops were much too busy to help.

At four o'clock in the morning, I finished transporting my explosives to the foot of the mountain. The sun had not yet risen on January 1, 1945. I had not slept since leaving Manila and had been running around the island ever since the boat landed; I was dead tired, so I lay down on the grass. Through the palm leaves I saw the sky growing lighter on this first day of the new year. A new year and a new job, I mused. And as I considered the stubbornness I was encountering, I heaved a deep sigh. I went to sleep there on the grass, my arms crossed on my chest.

I slept only about two hours, but when I awoke it was fully light. I jumped up and, facing east, bowed to the rising sun.

At about eight thirty in the morning on January 3, a lookout I had stationed at the top of the mountain came running toward me.

"Enemy fleet sighted!" he cried.

Clutching my binoculars, I hurried up the mountain. What the lookout had seen was an enemy fleet, all right. And what a fleet!

As carefully as I could, I counted the vessels. There were two battleships, four aircraft carriers, four cruisers and enough light cruisers and destroyers to make up a total of thirty-seven or thirty-eight warships. What astonished me most, however, was not this awesome armada, but the host of troop transports that followed it. There must have been nearly 150 of them. As if that were not enough, the sea was literally peppered with landing craft—more than I could possibly count.

The invasion of Luzon was about to begin.

I composed a cable giving the number of vessels of various

types that I had counted. Toward the end, I wrote, "Besides large vessels, there were innumerable landing craft and subchasers. They were bobbing so in the waves that I could not even make an estimate." I concluded, "Fleet headed north."

For some reason Lieutenant Hayakawa made a mistake and cabled "Fleet headed east," but I saw the message and quickly sent off a correction. If the fleet had actually been on an eastward course, it would have been heading straight toward Manila, but in fact the northern course was without doubt taking it to Lingayen Gulf.

I was not sure that this cable had been received until thirty years later, when I saw Major Taniguchi at Wakayama Point. The Lubang Garrison had only a small short-range radio transmitter of the kind used between battalions. For my message to reach army headquarters, it would have to go through a communications squad to regimental headquarters and then division headquarters, and be decoded and reworded at each step.

Thirty minutes after the message was dispatched, the Airfield Garrison caught a signal from naval headquarters ordering all units in western Luzon to take up battle stations, but we did not know whether this order was based on our warning or not.

I felt a certain amount of satisfaction at having carried out my first official duty, but I was far from happy, because I feared that a section might break off from the enemy's Luzon landing force and attack Lubang. If this happened, the attack would begin with a thorough drubbing by enemy artillery, and the explosives that I had brought to the mountain on the last day of the year would go up in smoke.

At my urging, Lieutenant Hayakawa put his troops on the alert and had them move my explosives farther inland. Fortunately, the entire enemy fleet continued on toward Lingayen Gulf; not a single ship came toward Lubang. At the same time, thanks to the arrival of this fleet, the *Seifuku* Maru never came back to our island.

If no boats were coming, there was no further need for the pier. Once again I asked to be allowed to demolish it, but Lieutenant Suehiro was still hesitant.

"Wait a little longer," he said. "When the time comes, I'll take steps to blow it up."

The man was trying to put the operation off just as long as he possibly could. The best I could get out of him was permission to let me use his troops to prepare for eventual demolition. I had them distribute the explosives still left on the pier in various strategic points and wired all the charges so that they could be detonated with a switch. In case the switch did not work, I strung out fuses.

A few days later two coded messages were received from division headquarters. The first said: "The Lubang Garrison is hereby placed directly under division command and will henceforth receive its orders directly from the division commander. Reports from the Lubang Garrison have an important bearing on the division's battle strategy. Henceforth you are to report directly and in detail to division communications headquarters."

Upon receipt of this message, the garrison requested additional code tables and a supply of batteries, but the only answer received was, "Two diesel boats commanded by two transport officers are missing. The garrison is to search the island and report whether they have landed there."

I had been told at division headquarters that unless I received word to the contrary before January 10, on that day I would become a full-fledged second lieutenant. No word came, and I assumed that my commission had become official, but during the next thirty years I never once wore a full officer's uniform.

On February 1, the enemy began landing operations at Nasugbu in west central Luzon. Nasugbu was on the shore opposite Lubang, and I reacted to this development by urging the garrison troops to move their food and ammunition farther up into the mountains.

I calculated that this operation would take about a week. As it turned out this was unrealistic, because only about half of the fifty men were available for work. Some were suffering from fatigue, some had fever; even the healthier ones could carry no more than about thirty-five pounds at a time.

To make matters worse, Lieutenant Hayakawa had had an attack of kidney trouble and needed to stop frequently to rest and take a drink of coconut milk. With their commander in this shape, the men were all the more truculent. It did not seem to me that they had any will to go on fighting.

The other outfits were no help. They began grumbling that if the enemy attacked, the garrison troops were supposed to stand in the front line and protect them as best they could. If the garrison was going to hide in the mountains, they said, they might as well commit suicide on the spot.

No matter how I tried, I could convince no one of the necessity for guerrilla warfare. They all talked big about committing suicide and giving up their lives for the emperor. Deep down they were hoping and praying that Lubang would not be attacked. I was sure of this, but there was nothing I could do about it. I had so little real authority that they did not even take me seriously.

My nickname among them was "Noda Shōyu," the name of a famous brand of soy sauce. The *Noda* came from my name and *Shōyu* was suggested by *shōi*, the word for second lieutenant. The meaning was that I was not the main course—only a bit of seasoning. Needless to say, this was because I could not actually issue orders to them in the same way as the commanders of their outfits.

How many times I wished that I were even a first lieutenant! Then maybe some of the work would get done. As it was, I had to listen to these men babbling at the mouth about dying for the cause, and listen silently with the knowledge that I was not permitted that out. I could not even hint to anyone that I had orders not to die. It was frustrating in the extreme.

I myself put off blowing up the airfield, because the project had ceased to have much meaning. I could crisscross the runway with ditches and potholes, but I had learned that the enemy now had steel plates with which they could make a new runway in no time. They used heavy beams under the plates, and as long as the terrain was roughly flat, holes in the ground were no hindrance. The most I could hope to gain from tearing up the field was a delay of a day or so, and it seemed to me that the explosives could be put to more effective use elsewhere.

As I was wondering what to do about the airfield, I remembered the famous fourteenth-century samurai Kusunoki Masashige, who during a difficult battle had a lot of straw men made and fitted out with helmets so as to waste precious enemy arrows. I decided to take a leaf out of Masashige's book. With Lieutenant Suehiro's assistance, I gathered up pieces of airplanes that had been destroyed and laid them out to look like new airplanes, taking care to camouflage them with grass.

As I think back on it, the scheme sounds rather childishly simple, but it worked. After that, when enemy planes came, they invariably strafed my decoys on the airfield. At that time, they were coming over every other day, and we utilized the other days to put together fake airplanes. I considered it good guerrilla tactics to make attacking planes waste as much ammunition as possible.

Around this time the Fifteenth and Sixteenth Coastal

Advance Squads arrived at the harbor in Tilik. These were army suicide squads that had small wooden boats, powered by automobile engines and loaded with explosives. The idea was that when an enemy ship appeared offshore, the squads would blow it up by ramming their boats into it. The two squads that came to Lubang were sent on the theory that the enemy would soon send a landing fleet to Manila, which they would be able to attack from the flank.

The Japanese forces had already abandoned Manila, and Fourteenth Area Army headquarters had moved to Baguio. The coastal advance squads, which consisted of forty men under the command of Captain Sadakichi Tsukii, arrived with no food, and the garrison had to divide its rice with them.

Before I arrived, the garrison had been sent a five-month supply of rice, and I urged the troops to stretch this out as far as possible. With the arrival of the extra men, I began to feel that we would not be able to hold out for very long, unless unusual measures were taken.

Acting on my own, I ordered the mayor of the town of Lubang to supply us with fifty sacks of polished rice. When the Suehiro and Ōsaki outfits found out about this, without saying anything to me they ordered the mayor to supply them with rice too. The mayor came weeping and said that if the islanders supplied all our demands, they would starve.

A check revealed that the other outfits had demanded two sacks per man; I talked them into reducing this to one sack, but after this incident the islanders would not listen to anything we said. They started complaining that they could not transport the rice in the daytime, because they might be killed by American planes. When we told them to do the work at night, they replied that they could only work when there was a moon, because otherwise they could not see what they were doing. This was nonsense. The truth of the matter was simply that they did not want to help the Japanese troops. With Manila surrounded by the enemy and American airborne troops landing on Corregidor, things were obviously going badly for Japan. The islanders were taking advantage of our helplessness.

If we let them carry this very far, we would not secure a sufficient supply of food before the enemy landed on our island. I ordered the rice bearers to use lamps if they had to. But then the mayor came again, protesting that they still could not move the rice because they had no fuel for lamps. I ordered him to mix the aviation fuel left on the island with lubrication oil and use that.

One way or another, I managed to conceal the rice supply in the mountains, but about that time the seventy men from the radar and air intelligence units piled in on us. They had received orders to act in conjunction with us in the future.

These were the troops who had stuck up their noses every time I had talked about guerrilla tactics, the ones who had waited for the last boat even though they already had orders to withdraw. Now that they were stranded, we had to take charge of them. There were forty of us already; with another seventy mouths, it was clear that what we had regarded as a five-month supply of rice would last barely two months.

Futhermore, some of the men took to stealing rice and swapping it with the Filipinos for sugar. San Jose had been a big sugar center, and refugees who had fled from there to Lubang after the enemy landed on Mindoro had brought a considerable supply with them. The Ōsaki unit foolishly took them up on their offer to trade one sack for two sacks of rice. One of Ōsaki's men even came to me and asked if the garrison did not want to get in on the deal.

I gave him a good dressing down, but even as I yelled at him, my heart was sinking. What can you do with a bunch of idiots?

After that came the coffee incident. Some time back a tanker had run aground off the coast of Tagbac, and the garrison had stored its cargo with the islanders. Now a group from the Ōsaki outfit broke into the islanders' houses and made off with a quantity of coffee. I called Corporal Suzuki, who was responsible for the men, and gave him a bawling-out, but the incident only depressed me further.

I had been sent to this island to fight, only to find that the troops I was supposed to lead were a bunch of good-for-nothings, quick to profess their willingness to die, but actually concerned only with their immediate wants. As if this were not enough, I had no authority to issue orders to them. I could only deploy them with the consent of their commander. I could have managed somehow if Lieutenant Hayakawa had delegated his command to me, but despite his serious illness, he refused to relinquish his authority. He had to pass on everything.

It was infuriating. There I was, powerless, with a disorderly pack of troops, none of whom understood the first thing about the kind of guerrilla war that we would soon be engaged in. I began to hope that the enemy would go ahead and land. At least that would clear the air!

The enemy obliged three days later.

THE FOUR-DAY BATTLE

On the west side of the island was a village called Tomibo, where a force of about fifty American soldiers landed on February 28.

I was on a mountaintop, which later became a radar base for the Philippine Air Force. Since this mountain was about five hundred yards high, we referred to it simply as Five Hundred. When I sighted the Americans with my binoculars, my whole body went tense, and I said aloud, "They've finally come!"

Disembarking from their landing craft, the American troops moved cautiously forward over the gently sloping terrain, their rifles ready. Something was wrong: there were not enough of them. It was a trick. Lubang is only a small island, and they may have known that it was not heavily defended, but even so the enemy would hardly attempt to take it with only fifty men. They were trying to trap us.

And Lieutenant Suehiro fell into the trap. Speaking with gusto, he said, "I'll take a few men over there and wipe them out."

"Don't do it," I urged. "You can bank on it that they are about to land in force at another point. Let's just wait a while and see what happens."

"Don't worry, Lieutenant! Fifty or a hundred Yanks don't amount to a fart. We'll wipe them out in no time."

And he jumped onto his truck with about fifteen men. They had one heavy machine gun, and each of the men had an infantry rifle. Tomibo was only about two miles from the top of Five Hundred as the crow flies, but there was no road between them. Lieutenant Suehiro decided to take the road along the north coast and around the west end of the island. This was quite a detour, but it would give the lieutenant a chance to look in on his sick troops in the town of Lubang on the way.

Keeping our voices down, we began to prepare our defenses. In the rolling hills considerably down the mountain from where we were, the air intelligence squad, which had a radar set, had dug in, along with part of the air maintenance crew.

The Americans had disappeared into the forest this side of the beach, and at sunset we had neither seen nor heard any more of them. Where were they? And what was Lieutenant Suehiro doing? I grew more nervous as time went on. By nightfall I was beginning to feel that the enemy was breathing down my back.

Night enveloped us in inky darkness. It had been a long day. At about one o'clock in the morning a truck drove up, and Lieutenant Ōsaki jumped out, followed by Warrant Officer Tachibana. They had brought the part of the maintenance crew that had been left at the airfield. But no sign of Lieutenant Suehiro.

Warrant Officer Tachibana explained, "Lieutenant Suehiro stayed in Lubang. He tried to persuade us to stay, but we thought it was too dangerous. We decided to come here."

Not thirty minutes later we saw flames rising in the vicinity of Lubang. I felt certain the Suehiro group had come under enemy fire, but there was no way to make sure. I was more nervous than ever. I do not know how many times I must have grasped the handle of my sword.

As dawn broke, I aimed my binoculars toward Tilik, and sure enough, in the offing I spotted an enemy light cruiser and three troop transports making straight for the island. I decided to smoke a cigarette to calm myself. It took me five or six matches to light it. Then I thought of the incense tube I had snitched from my father. I did not want that to fall into an enemy hand, so I burned it, along with my secret papers.

The naval ships began their bombardment—ear-splitting shots followed by thunderous explosions as the shells found their mark. My whole insides shook with the vibrations. Tilik was the enemy's chief target, and in no time the coast in that direction was covered with dust and smoke. Palm trees and parts of houses flew through the air, as the little town of Tilik disappeared before our eyes. The bombardment went on relentlessly. Our base was so far away that I was not really frightened, but I worried about the coastal advance squads. Their little attack boats had been hidden in the river that empties into Tilik Bay, ready to launch an attack as soon as enemy ships appeared, but the enemy, perhaps on guard against such an attack was pouring volley after volley into the little river.

And what about the pier? I had lined it with explosives, but I could not tell whether it had been blown up or not.

After about two hours the bombardment finally ended, but as soon as it stopped, shells from enemy land mortars began raining down on our encampment. We hid as best we could behind trees. Enemy planes swooped down, dropping two-hundred-pound parachute bombs. Swinging back and forth from their chutes, they sort of fluttered down to earth and then erupted with an unearthly noise. The more I looked, the angrier I became. The enemy obviously knew we had no antiaircraft weapons.

Finally the planes went away. I looked through my binoculars and saw that the light cruiser, flying the Stars and Stripes, was advancing toward Tilik harbor. The troop transports were also under way.

At that point, a soldier from Lieutenant Suehiro's outfit

came crawling up the mountain. He reported that during the previous night the outfit's quarters in the town had been attacked.

"We were caught in a real crossfire. Everybody but me . . ." He broke off.

"Are they all dead? What about Lieutenant Suehiro?"

"He was standing by the window. They got him first thing."

Just as I feared, the fire in the town the night before had been Lieutenant Suehiro's barracks. Although the lieutenant and I had had our disagreements, it hurt inside to know he was gone. I remembered how he had rushed about helping me put together my fake airplanes.

When the bombardment began, Lieutenant Ueno of the Sixteenth Coastal Attack Squad ordered his men to take shelter in the mountains but stayed behind himself to blow up the engines of the attack boats. He soon realized that the enemy was pointing artillery directly at him. There being no chance of surviving, he too beat a retreat into the mountains. When I heard his story, I could hardly believe it. Machine guns, even mortars, yes, but naval guns against a single enemy straggler? Incredible! The enemy must have equipment and ammunition to throw away!

Presently the troops landed—a battalion of marines led by four tanks. Looking out from among the trees, I saw them march off toward Vigo, a mile or two west of Tilik. Just before they reached Vigo, they split into two units. One unit continued westward toward the town of Lubang, while the other started advancing toward our base. I decided on a retreat. If we dug in and made a stand where we were, we did not have the remotest chance of winning. I figured that the only chance left was to go up into the mountains and carry on a guerrilla campaign.

The intelligence squad and the coastal attack squads did not agree. They said they would hold out to the end where they were. I tried to tell them that with no more armaments than they had, they would be sitting ducks for the enemy, but they would not listen.

Enemy shells began to fall, and I ordered the wounded soldiers who were able to walk to move deeper into the mountains. Picking out five or six strong-looking men, I ordered them to carry as many provisions as they could, and we started off.

We had not walked for thirty minutes when we heard guns from the direction in which we were moving. The enemy had apparently cut off our retreat. I had been afraid of something like this. Some time before I had told the Ōsaki outfit that instead of waiting around for planes to come to the rescue, they should get busy and move provisions to the rear, so that when the attack did come they could fall back and make a stand.

If they had paid any attention then, we would not be in the position we were in now. I sent a lookout ahead, then set out myself with a small force. Before long we met the lookout, limping back with a bullet wound in his leg. He had been spotted by an enemy scout. It was now certain that our retreat was cut off, no doubt by the troops who had landed in Tomibo the day before.

In front of us, the enemy's mortars were coming closer. We were trapped! Suddenly I noticed blood on the path; bending down to take a look, I sighted two Japanese soldiers lying on their stomachs a little ahead of us. They were Private First Class Kinshichi Kozuka and Private First Class Muranaka. I called to them to creep forward a little farther. Muranaka looked at Kozuka for a moment, then for some crazy reason stood straight up. Instantly a shot rang out, and he fell. The bullet had hit him in the head.

Shouting to Kozuka to stay down, I crawled backward a little, and feeling around with my foot, I found a ditch. Suddenly, the light-footed Kozuka was up and running toward me. He jumped over me into the ditch, just as another shot rang out. I slipped back into the ditch before noticing that my right hand was covered with blood. The bullet had sliced off the tip of my little finger, leaving only a little of the nail.

On the following night I resolved to carry out a raid on the troops blocking our retreat.

Lieutenant Ōsaki had been killed yesterday, Lieutenant Tanaka today, both by mortar shells. Together with Lieutenant Suehiro, we had lost three officers, and another, Lieutenant Tategami, was missing, having gone off in pursuit of enemy scouts (he was later found dead). With no commanding officers, the troops lost all sense of organization. They were firing willy-nilly, as the spirit moved them. Unless something was done soon, they would all be destroyed.

A mountain range, about eighteen hundred feet high at its peak and covered with dense forest, ran down the island from northwest to southeast. My idea was to retreat along the ridge, offering resistance when necessary. I thought that if we could reach a certain point I had in mind, some of us could then double back along the skirt of the mountains to our former base, where provisions had been hidden, and then dive back into the forest.

To carry out this plan, it was essential to wipe out the enemy troops to the rear. I waited until the night of March 2, because Captain Tsukii had promised to rendezvous with me by that time at the latest. His squad had almost no weapons; I did not want to retreat ahead of them, leaving them defenseless.

Holding up under sporadic mortar fire, we waited and waited, but no Captain Tsukii. I finally decided we could wait no longer. Taking fifteen men with me, I set out to attack the enemy troops who were blocking us. The path along the ridge was fairly straight, and if we were to run into the enemy, the men in the vanguard would certainly be wounded or killed. Still, I figured that if we resigned ourselves to sacrificing three or four men, the rest of us could get through to the enemy camp. I was confident that in hand-to-hand combat we would beat them.

The airfield had been captured intact by the enemy. The pier had not been blown up. I had, in short, allowed the enemy to land without accomplishing either of the specific objectives I had been assigned by division headquarters. I had disgraced myself as a secret warfare agent. Deep down I felt that we would not be in the predicament we were in if I had been more forceful and aggressive as a leader. The only way I could see now to discharge my duty to those who had died so tragically was to carry out this desperate night attack on the enemy. I would lead the way into the enemy camp and slaughter as many Americans as I could.

When we reached a certain point, I took a deep breath and looked around behind me. The men's helmets dully reflected the moonlight. I breathed again and drew my sword, discarding the scabbard by the wayside. From now on I would not think of anything. I grasped the sword tightly and started forward. I had nothing to rely on but my own strength.

When I threw away my scabbard, I was disobeying the orders I had received from General Yokoyama. I was also ignoring all I had been taught at Futamata about the duties of a secret warfare agent. I was reverting instead to the suicide tactics I had been taught at officers' training school. I was young; I had lost my head!

If the enemy had been waiting for us at that moment, I would probably have been killed. As luck would have it, however, they had found out about our night attack and withdrawn far to the rear. I was both crestfallen and relieved. We moved quickly back the way we had come.

On the way we found the body of Private First Class Muranaka. With the dagger my mother had given me, I cut off his little finger, which I wrapped in paper and placed in the inner pocket of my jacket. I also recovered my scabbard. As I picked it up, I remembered the division commander's face as he ordered me to stay alive. I was ashamed of myself.

On the morning of the third, Captain Tsukii and his men finally arrived at our base. I decided to check our path of retreat once more, and I took Corporal Shōichi Shimada with me. As we started to leave, Lieutenant Ueno told me he had also sent out a scout and asked me to bring him back if I saw him.

Then, just as we were setting out from the base, a messenger came from the sick tent asking for explosives. I went to the tent to see what the situation was. A young man with a very pale face looked up at me from his cot and mumbled, "We can't move. Please let us kill ourselves here."

The rest of the twenty men in the tent, all gravely wounded, stared pitifully at me.

I suppressed my emotions and said, "All right, I'll do it. I'll attach a fuse to set off the dynamite, but just in case it doesn't, I'll leave a cannister, which you can throw into the dynamite to ignite it."

I looked at each and every face, twenty-two in all. They were all resigned to death, ready to make the sacrifice they had been brought up to make. With difficulty, I continued.

"Also, in the event that your matches don't light, I'm leaving a piece of long-burning incense to light the fuse with. One way or another, you should be able to achieve your wish. There is one thing, however, that I must ask you in return. It is hard for me to give you an assignment when you have already made up your minds to die, but I ask you one more time—just one more time—to serve your country. Do not blow yourselves up until you can see the enemy from this tent. There is food here. You can hold on until the enemy has been sighted."

One man answered, "It's all the same to us whether the enemy comes or not."

"I know that, but it's not the same to us. If the enemy invades this base, we can't return to it. We want some way of knowing whether the enemy has come or not. Do you understand?"

They said they understood and would do as I requested. Then they all thanked me for making it possible for them to destroy themselves.

I prepared the explosives and the cannister and left the tent.

The feeble voices followed me, "Take care of yourself, Commander!"

I found Corporal Shimada and pushed off.

Later I came back to the place and found no trace of either the tent or the twenty-two corpses. Nothing was left but a gaping hole in the ground. I stood there and stared at it. I did not think to bow my head or say a prayer. I just stood and stared at that awful hole. Even the tears refused to come.

After Shimada and I had walked for a while, we ran into the scout that Lieutenant Ueno had mentioned. He was a boy of only seventeen or eighteen. I asked him whether he had sighted enemy troops; he said no.

"Go back to the base," I told him. "Guide the men there to the point where we are now. In the meantime, we'll check the road ahead and take up a guard position there. When you've brought the troops here and secured the place, come ahead for us. Whatever happens, see that you establish contact with us."

After seeing him off, Shimada and I moved on, but we found no sign of the enemy. After a time, we decided to stop and wait for the young scout. If we went any farther, it would be impossible to return to the others before dark.

We waited one hour, two hours, but the boy did not show

up. The sun began to set, and I was worried. In the dark we had nothing to fear from the enemy, but it would be next to impossible to establish contact with our own men.

Shimada looked closely at my face and asked, "What shall we do, Lieutenant?"

I did not know the answer. If we started back now, it would be dark before we arrived. On the other hand, we had brought nothing at all to eat, and we were out of water.

Finally I said, "Before it gets too dark, let's go down into the valley and find some water." We clambered down about 150 yards into a ravine and found a brook, but as we were making our way back up, the sun set, and we found ourselves in total darkness.

"Where are you, Lieutenant?" asked Shimada.

"I'm still here," I replied.

It was so dark that we had to keep reassuring each other that we were still together, but we pressed on in an effort to find the ridge again.

That was a mistake. After a while, we realized that we were going in circles. We decided to sit down and wait until morning.

At dawn we started out again, and before long we spotted the place where we had been the evening before. From among the trees, I looked out at the road and got the shock of my life. Not one hundred feet away was an American scouting party!

Shimada had a rifle, but I had only a pistol and my sword. We were hopelessly outmatched. We threw hand grenades simultaneously and the instant they went off scrambled down into the valley. After crawling around down there for about thirty minutes, we cautiously worked our way back up to a point just below the spot where our young scout had been instructed to lead our men. Feeling fairly sure that it would be safe this time, we started up the cliff above us, and almost immediately found ourselves in a shower of mortar shells. They arced up into the sky one after another, landing in the valley below us. We hugged the cliff, not daring to move.

The young scout had followed my orders and brought the troops to the appointed place, where they had set up their machine guns and spent the night. In the morning, the enemy scouting party we had seen appeared, and our troops opened fire on them with machine guns, killing one American. The other enemy soldiers withdrew, but almost immediately there was a barrage of mortar fire.

I did not know all this until later, of course. The shells Shimada and I saw falling in the valley were misses from the barrage aimed at the men on the hill. Misses or not, they were falling all over the valley, and there was nothing we could do but stay where we were.

Finally the firing ceased, and quiet returned, but we were afraid to go up the hill immediately. The silence itself had an eerie quality. The sky above was a transparent blue. There was not a cloud to be seen.

Something else I did not find out until later was that while we were on the cliff, Captain Tsukii had ordered the men to disperse. He sent some toward Vigo and some in the direction of Tilik. When we reached the top of the crest, there was nobody there. I decided to go back to our former barracks, where supplies had been cached. It seemed likely to me that any Japanese troops would eventually go there for food.

On the way I saw American chewing gum wrappers by the side of the road. In one place a wad of chewing gum was sticking to the leaf of a weed. Here we were holding on for dear life, and these characters were chewing gum while they fought! I was more sad than angry. The chewing gum tinfoil told me just how miserably we had been beaten.

Any semblance of organized warfare on Lubang ended that day. Afterward there were only occasional mopping-up operations by the enemy.

Lieutenant Hayakawa was attacked in the upper reaches of the Vigo River while he was taking a break after eating. He and ten of his men were killed.

Captain Tsukii and the Fifteenth Coastal Attack Squad attempted to storm the enemy barracks at Tilik, but failed. They were later attacked on the Vigo River and again on the south coast. In the meantime, Captain Tsukii fell ill and died.

I heard that Lieutenant Ueno and the Sixteenth Coastal Attack Squad also launched an unsuccessful raid in the Tilik area and later hid in the hills south of the port, but I had no further word from them. So far as I could tell I was the only Japanese officer left on the island.

The only men I was able to communicate with were ten members of the garrison unit, four members of the air intelligence squad, four members of the air maintenance crew and two members of the navy squad—twenty in all. The only army noncoms left were Corporal Shimada and Corporal Yoshio Fujita.

One day Corporal Fujita picked up a model 99 infantry rifle in the woods. I had earlier found a model 38, and I traded it to Fujita for the model 99, because I had about three hundred cartridges for a 99. I carried this model 99 for the remainder of my thirty years on Lubang.

I hoped eventually to lead the troops in an attack on the airfield, and I ordered them to stretch out the rice supply as long as possible. It was March, and I calculated that if each man ate four bowls a day, we could hold out until August. But the soldiers were more worried about their own bellies than about anything else, and some of them took to filching rice from the storage bins. At mealtimes they griped over the tiniest difference between their helping and the next person's; sometimes they would have come to blows if I had not stopped them. If the enemy had ever attacked us at mealtime, we would have been wiped out on the spot.

Just as I was wondering what to do to maintain order, Corporal Fujita said to me, "I don't think it is safe for us all to be in one place. We might be surrounded at any time. Would you permit some of us to split off and go somewhere else?"

I immediately consented. I knew that I could not rely on this motley crew of soldiers who had given themselves over to being pigs. I also knew, however, the real reason why some of them wanted to leave. It was not that they feared encirclement. That was only an excuse. What they really wanted was their share of the remaining rice.

As if this were not apparent, Fujita said, "If we split off from the group, each of us will have to have a supply of food."

"That's right," I replied, "but I can't allot it all to the men who are here right now. There may still be others on the island who will come here to get food. Everyone knew this was the place where the provisions were hidden."

I decided upon their allotment and ordered them absolutely not to take more, though I knew then that they would probably find a way to do so. I also told them always to stay in groups of three or more. If there are three, two can stand guard front and rear while the other prepares the rice for meals.

And so we broke up into cells. I joined up with Corporal Shimada and one private. The others split into four small groups, each man deciding for himself which of his friends he wanted to stick with.

After a time I decided that my group should move to a new location, and on April 18 we started transferring supplies. We were in the midst of this when an enemy clean-up squad stormed into the woods firing like crazy. The private, apparently paralyzed by the guns, stood rooted to the spot and was killed. Of the men in the other groups, only Kozuka ever showed up at the place where Shimada and I were camped, and that was sometime later. Shimada and I were therefore alone for a while.

After the attack, Kozuka went to join some of the air intelligence squad. He soon came down with acute nephritis, however, and the others left him. After wandering around in the foothills for about a week, living on potato vines and coconut milk, he recovered enough to make his way to where Shimada and I were. After that the three of us were together.

Around the middle of May, for the first time in some weeks, we heard the sound of mortars and machine guns. It was coming from the vicinity of Binacas, on the south shore. We just looked at each other—there was no need to speak. One of the other groups had been discovered and surrounded.

I found out later that a group of survivors from Captain Tsukii's squad had made their way to Binacas and were resting there when they were attacked by the enemy. All were killed but two, who by some miracle managed to flee. One of them told me that during the attack two of Captain Tsukii's subordinates stood up waving their pistols and shouted "Banzai to the Emperor!" before being gunned down.

We referred to this incident as the "May Suppression Campaign." It was the last organized enemy attack on Japanese survivors, but afterward an enemy squad patrolled the ridge every morning, occasionally firing a few menacing shots.

It was around the middle of October that I first saw one of the leaflets urging us to surrender. A group of Japanese had killed a cow in the mountains and were taking it back to their camp when they met five or six islanders. One of them started to pull a bolo knife but gave up when he saw that the Japanese had guns. The islanders fled, leaving behind them a piece of paper. Printed on it in Japanese was a statement saying "The war ended on August 15. Come down from the mountains!"

Neither I nor the others believed this, because just a few days before a group of Japanese who had gone to kill a cow had bumped into an enemy patrol and had immediately been fired on. How could that happen if the war was over?

After we split into cells, we lived in the woods on the slopes of the mountains. We set up little tents and spread boards on the ground to sleep on. My group at least was trying to stretch out its rice supply, and sometimes we were able to supplement the rice with bananas or meat from a cow we had killed.

The groups stayed in touch with each other and occasionally exchanged reports, but I refused to tell the other groups where our tent was. My orders to carry out a guerrilla campaign came directly from the division commander, and I could not be bothered with the groups who were thinking of nothing but food. To the best of my ability I was trying to study the terrain so that I could be useful when the Japanese army launched its counterattack. It was necessary for me to remain alive, and to live with a group of disorderly, irresponsible soldiers was simply to invite danger.

I told neither Corporal Shimada nor Private First Class Kozuka of my special mission. I did not know whether they were reliable, nor could I tell yet how capable they were.

From May until August, enemy patrols came into the mountains daily, and we could hear shots from their guns. After the middle of August they stopped coming. Still, we frequently heard shots from the lower reaches of the mountains, and it appeared that the enemy had control of the accesses. I thought this meant that they were trying to starve us out.

We saw our second surrender leaflet around the end of the year. A Boeing B-17 flew over our hideout and dropped a lot of big, thick pieces of paper. On the front were printed the surrender order from General Yamashita of the Fourteenth Area Army and a directive from the chief of staff. On the back was a map of Lubang on which the place where the leaflets were dropped was marked with a circle.

We gathered together and considered whether the orders printed on the leaflet were genuine. I had my doubts about a sentence saying that those who surrendered would be given "hygienic succor" and "hauled" to Japan.

Somebody said, "What's 'hygienic succor'? I never heard of it."

Somebody else mused, "They're going to 'haul' us to Japan? We aren't cargo, are we?"

What bothered me from the very first was that General Yamashita's command purported to have been issued in accordance with a "Direct Imperial Order." I had never heard of a "Direct Imperial Order." An intelligence squad man, who had been through law school, said he had never heard of one either.

There were other suspicious features. For example, a close reading of the text suggested that General Yamashita was issuing the order to himself, among other officers. I later found out that this was simply a printer's error, but at the time I could only conclude that the leaflet was phony. The others all agreed with me. There was no doubt in our minds that this was an enemy trick.

THE VOW TO FIGHT ON

We began a new year, 1946. This meant that I had been on Lubang for a full twelve months. On New Year's morning we bowed to the rising sun and swore to do our best in the coming year.

We rarely heard guns anymore, but every once in a while we were frightened by machine gun fire, apparently directed at the mountains where we were hiding. I saw an aircraft carrier off the coast, and Grummon fighters passed over from time to time. Obviously the war was still going on.

At the beginning of February, Corporal Shimada went hunting with Eishichi Irizawa and Shōji Kobayashi of the garrison squad and a soldier named Watanabe from the air intelligence squad. They found no game, and after parting from Watanabe, who was returning by a different route, they started back empty-handed toward our base.

During the daytime they had seen some Philippine soldiers in a truck at the bottom of the mountains, but it did not occur to them that the soldiers were coming into the woods on the mountainside. Chatting and laughing as they made their way back, they suddenly discovered that they had entered the Philippine soldiers' bivouac. The Filipinos, startled to see Japanese troops, thought they were being attacked and immediately opened fire. Corporal Shimada dived into the nearby bushes and escaped down a hill, but both Irizawa and Kobayashi were killed.

Very shortly after that, Private First Class Yūichi Akatsu joined the three of us. He had been camping with Irizawa and Kobayashi, but their death left him all alone. You could tell from looking at him that he was a weakling, and Kozaka tried to send him away.

"Go somewhere else," he urged. "You can't keep up with us. Your body is weak, and you don't know much about soldiering. We can't use you. Go over to Corporal Fujita's group."

Akatsu said he would, but he kept hanging on to us, because we had more food than any of the others. The other groups were almost out of rice; they kept coming to ask us to give them some. I gave them all the same answer: "You men made pigs of yourselves when you had rice, so now you don't have any. Don't come asking me to give you any of ours. I was sent here to destroy the airfield, and I still plan to do it. We're eating as little rice as possible. We fill out our diet with bananas and meat, and that's what you should have been doing. If we give you rice, we'll all be in trouble. You don't know how to conserve."

Afterward it occurred to me that my refusal to supply the others with rice might have been what caused them to surrender, as forty-one of them, including Corporal Fujita, did in April.

After March there were more and more leaflets urging us to surrender, and from time to time we heard people calling to us in Japanese. Later on, the Japanese who had surrendered began leaving notes for us saying, "Nobody is searching for you now but Japanese. Come on out!"

But we could not believe that the war had really ended. We thought the enemy was simply forcing prisoners to go along with their trickery. Every time the searchers called out to us, we moved to a different location.

I grew accustomed to their pleas. "Lieutenant Onoda," they would say, "we have established contact with the search party. Please come out. We're now at Point X, combing this whole area. Please come to this point."

They dropped leaflets written in pencil in good Japanese, which made a deep impression on Private First Class Akatsu. One evening after we had eaten, he said, "Lieutenant, don't you suppose the war really has ended?"

When I replied that I did not, Shimada said, "I sort of have a feeling that it has, too."

Kozuka remained silent. After studying their faces for a moment, I said, "All right, if that's what the three of you think, I'll go and make sure. All three of you have 38s. Even if you lose two of them, you'll still be able to use the ammunition. If I lose my 99, however, the ammunition will go to waste. I'll leave it here and take only hand grenades with me. I should be back soon. If things are the way Akatsu says, I'll go out into the open with you. But if I don't come back, you'll know that the war is still going on. You can decide for yourselves then whether you want to fight to the end or not."

My real intention was to try to rescue the Japanese who had been taken prisoner. A lot of them must have been tricked into surrendering by other Japanese whom the enemy was using as pawns. I thought that if I could get into the prison where they were, I could foment some kind of disturbance, and we could all escape together.

The enemy must have heard from their prisoners that I had come to Lubang to engage in guerrilla warfare. They would see through my sham surrender and no doubt clamp handcuffs on me immediately. That meant I would have to act fast. If I failed, I would be killed, but if I succeeded, we would get back quite a few men. Once again I was preparing to ignore the division commander's orders and risk death, just as I had when I threw away my scabbard and launched a suicide attack.

At this point Kozuka spoke up.

"Wait a minute, Lieutenant! Why do you have to take the responsibility? Didn't everybody agree with you about that 'Direct Imperial Order'? You probably think it reflects on your honor that the others got taken prisoner because of a phony leaflet. I don't think it's your fault.

"I'll stay on with you. I'll fight to the end. If these two cowards want to surrender, let's let them do it!"

I nodded to Kozuka and said, "Do you mean it? Will you stay? If you will, I have nothing more to say. I don't really want to take responsibility for that bunch of nimcompoops that let themselves get captured. You yourself haven't said anything up till now, so I was wondering whether you wanted to surrender too. If you're willing to go on, I'll go on too."

In the back of my mind I thought of General Yokoyama telling me that as long as I had one soldier, I was to lead him even if we had to live on coconuts.

"Lieutenant," said Shimada quietly, "I'll go on with you too."

The three of us automatically looked at Akatsu, who said in a low voice, "I'll go on too, if that's what you're going to do."

And so the four of us vowed to each other to keep on fighting. It was early April, 1946, and by this time we four made up the only Japanese resistance left on Lubang.

At the time, Corporal Shimada, the oldest of us, was thirty-one. Kozuka was twenty-five, and Akatsu twenty-three. On my last birthday, which was March 19, I had turned twenty-four.

We four were always moving from one place to another on the island. The enemy might attack at any time. It was dangerous to stay in one place very long.

During the first year we slept crowded together in our little tent, even in the rainy season.

The rainy season in Lubang lasted from July until mid October. Often when the rain came down in buckets all night long, it did no good to stay huddled up in the tent. We still got soaked to the bone. Our skin would turn white, and we would shiver from the cold, even though it was summer. Often I felt like screaming out in protest.

But how wonderful it was when the rain stopped! We would fall all over each other to get out of the tent, then stand there stretching each numb finger. I remember how I welcomed the sight of the stars through the clouds.

Corporal Shimada, the only one of us who was married, was of a naturally cheerful disposition. He always had something to talk about, and he took the lead when we sat around chatting in the evening. Tall and well filled out, he was the best shot of the four. He said he had won an award at a shooting contest held by his company, and I saw no reason to doubt this. His hometown was Ogawa in Saitama Prefecture, not far northwest of Tokyo. He came from a farming family, and in the off season he had gone to the mountains to burn charcoal. In the area where he lived, young men were often sent up into the mountain for a month or so at a time to tend a charcoal kiln. Living alone in little huts, they learned to fend for themselves. Shimada taught me how to weave the straw sandals known as *waraji*. These were ideal footgear for the life we led, because we constantly had to make our way across rough or swampy territory.

Kozuka, who was even slighter of build than I, was very reticent. Only rarely did he speak without having been spoken to. On those occasions when he did loosen up, he talked with great feeling about the days before he entered the army, but even then he had trouble expressing himself. He was the son of a farmer in Hachiōji, a distant suburb of Tokyo, and I gathered that his family was fairly well-off. He said he had owned a racehorse.

Kozuka asked me what I had done before I went into the army. "I worked in the Hankow branch of a Japanese trading company," I replied. "My brother was an army lieutenant stationed in Hankow at the time, and I used to cadge money from him so I could go to a dance hall and dance all night."

They had trouble believing that I could dance, let alone that I had been something of a playboy in the cosmopolitan city of Hankow. I did not blame them. At this point I had trouble believing it myself.

Akatsu was the weakest of us, both physically and morally. He said he was the son of a shoemaker in the poorer quarters of Tokyo, and I suppose it was unfair to judge him by the side of two healthy farm boys. But without doubt he was a liability for us. When we brushed up against the enemy, he was always the one who fell behind or lost track of the others. I concluded that Kozuka had been right not to want him with us.

Living together the way we were, we had to adjust everything to the capabilities of the weakest. In dividing up the work we tried to take into account each man's strength, as well as his likes and dislikes. Shimada did most of the hard physical labor, Akatsu took charge of such chores as gathering firewood or bringing water from the nearest brook, and Kozuka and I made tools, stood guard, and planned our overall movements. When someone was in poor physical condition, we tried to lighten his load. We were conscious that we must avoid dissipating our physical strength.

Since I had the highest rank, I was officially the leader, but never once did I try to impose an order arbitrarily. It was all in all a cooperative effort.

I kept a constant eye on the physical condition of the other three. The important point was to maintain balance. It would not do to ask too much of any one man. The other three understood this and helped each other out cheerfully enough when the need arose.

At that time, each man had an infantry rifle, mine a 99 and the other three 38s. We each had two hand grenades and two pistols. There were three hundred cartridges for the 99 and nine hundred for the 38s. In addition, we had six hundred Lewis machine gun cartridges, which we later fixed so that they could be used in the 99.

We started with a three-month supply of rice, which we stretched out as long as possible. For a time we ate so little that it was difficult to force ourselves to move from one spot to another. When our own rice was gone, we went and found the rice that had been hidden for other Japanese troops remaining on the island. Before very long, that too was gone. And the islanders came and stole one of the two drums of rice the other forty-one men had left behind when they surrendered.

As soon as the Americans landed, the islanders went over to their side. They often acted as guides for the enemy, and we took great care to steer clear of them. After our number was reduced to four, they considered it safe enough to come in droves to the mountains to cut timber. They carried bolo knives at their side, and one person in the group always had a gun. We were more leery of them than we were of enemy patrols.

Whenever we caught sight of islanders, we hid. If they spotted us, we fired shots to scare them away, then moved our camp to a different spot as quickly as possible, because we knew they would report us.

When we sensed that any of them might be around, we hid in the bushes to avoid being seen, but no matter how cautious we were, they occasionally caught sight of us. When that happened, there was nothing to do but fire without hesitation and then run. Such encounters occurred three or four times during the first year.

When they came to the mountains to work, they brought uncooked rice and cooked it as they needed it, often leaving some in sacks hanging from trees for use on their next trip. These sacks of rice might have been classed as a gift from heaven but for the trouble involved in stealing them. We could not just walk off with a sack when we found one, because its disappearance was sure to reveal that we were in the vicinity.

Whenever we came across some of this rice, we first tried to ascertain how long it had been there. Since the islanders cooked the rice on the spot, there were always traces of a fire. We could tell from the ashes roughly how long ago the fire had been built. We would also examine the stumps of the trees the islanders had cut. If the woodcutters had been here only a day earlier, the stump was still damp, and there were usually green leaves lying about. If the stump was dry and the leaves had withered, we knew that more time had elapsed.

Footprints were an important aid, because we could often see that a set of footprints had been smeared by last night's shower or the heavy rain we had had three days ago, and we would know that the woodcutters had been here before that. If they left food, it meant that they were coming back. The question was how soon. Whenever we took the rice, we had to move to a new location. Since that took time, even if we were half-starved, we had to decide whether we would have enough time to make a getaway before they came back.

The northern part of Lubang was a gentle plain, but on the southern side, other than three or four small sandy beaches, there were only rugged, sea-torn cliffs.

The population of the island was about twelve thousand, most of whom were farmers living on the north side. Only a few fishermen lived in the south. Largely because of Akatsu's physical weakness, we centered our movements on the less populated, and therefore safer, mountains toward the south. We had a number of more or less fixed campsites, to which we gave names like "Twin Mountains" and "Two House Point," but we were afraid to stay in any of them very long.

Gradually, we developed a circuit of sorts, around which we moved from point to point, staying nowhere very long. This circuit was a rough ellipse coursing around the mountains in the central sector of the island (*see endpaper*). Starting at Gontin and moving counterclockwise, the next stop was Two House Point (or Kainan Point), then Wakayama Point, then Twin Mountains (or Kozuka Hill), then Shiokara Valley (or Shingu Point), then Snake Mountain Abutment (Kumano Point), then Five Hundred (later the radar base), then Binacas, then Six Hundred Peak and finally Gontin again. Sometimes when we reached Binacas we turned around and started back the other way.

We usually stayed in one place from three to five days. When we went fast, we covered the whole circuit in as little as a month, but usually it took about two months, so that in the eight-month dry season, we did about four circuits.

The amount of time we spent in one place depended to some extent on the availability of food. When there turned out to be more food somewhere than we had expected and little danger of being discovered by the islanders, naturally we lengthened our stay.

We carried all our belongings with us, dividing up the load equally. When we moved, we tried always to take along enough food for the next day, but sometimes we ran out and had to count on finding food at the next stop. The average load that each man had to carry was about forty-five pounds.

Although I had a pencil that I had found, I kept all the reports I intended to make in my head. I firmly believed that when friendly troops eventually established contact with us, they would need my reports in planning a counterattack. Their first objective would be to recapture the airfield, and I made mental notes about that area, as well as about the central part of the island where we were now living.

Since I returned to Japan, there has been some speculation

in the press as to whether I was left by the Japanese army as a spy, but I do not consider that I was a spy. I was sent to conduct guerrilla warfare, which is not the same thing. Cut off from the Japanese forces and reduced to the circumstances our group was in, there was no way for us to engage in guerrilla warfare in the ordinary sense. I could only perform those functions of guerrilla warfare that resemble the work of a spy.

The techniques I had been taught at Futamata were of little use to me. I had learned to tap telephone lines, open letters surreptitiously and undo handcuffs, but these all involved there being a lot of other people around. Here in these mountains, it was far more important to know how to build a fire without making much smoke. My course at Futamata had done nothing to fit me for a primitive life in the mountains, where the greatest enemy was nature. Shimada was better equipped for this because of his experience at burning charcoal. I learned a lot from him about the art of staying alive. He knew, for instance, how to make a net, and Kozuka and I were always searching for bits of string for him.

In Lubang, besides the cows raised by the islanders for meat, there were wild water buffaloes, wild boars, wild chickens and iguana ranging up to three feet in length. In hunting for food, we aimed mainly at the islanders' cows.

Our supply of ammunition was limited, and we had to use it as effectively as possible. The object was always to kill with a single shot. Two bullets for one cow would mean one less cow in the long run.

When we found food, we brought it all to one place for storage, and I meted out each day's portion. But as time went on, it seemed as though every time I went to the storage place, there was less there than there ought to have been. I knew why. Shimada and Akatsu were sneaking in and taking the food. Every time it happened, I spoke to them about it, but to little effect.

One day Kozuka complained strongly to me, "If we continue
to let this go on, I'm going to die. From now on, I'm going
to eat all I want too."

Bananas were our principal staple. There were banana fields
here and there all over the island, but we had to be careful
not to harvest too many. With a war of endurance in mind,
I had set up a long-range plan in which I had calculated the
amount of bananas to be harvested. If I allowed things to go
on as they were, there was a very real danger that the plan
would break down, and we would be destroyed from within.
The fact of the matter was that we were all suffering from
malnutrition.

Finally, I had had all I could stand.

"From now on." I decreed, "we'll keep our food separately.
Do not touch anyone else's food. That is absolutely forbidden."

It goes without saying that in those days eating was our
only pleasure. What we ate largely determined how well we
would feel on the following day. It would have been unfair in
these circumstances to blame anyone too severely for giving
in to his appetite. We had vowed to fight to the end, but as
time went on, it was all we could do to keep out of sight of the
islanders. Maybe it was only natural that animal instincts came
to the surface.

Still, as the person technically in charge, it was my responsibility to see that some restraints remained in force. I myself
would have liked to eat all I wanted. I would have liked to
sleep all I wanted to, too. But even aside from the shortage of
food, if we ate all we wanted, we would get fat, making it
harder than ever to do the work we had to do. And if we did
not develop the habit of suppressing our baser instincts, we
would gradually become demoralized to the point of admitting
to ourselves that we were stragglers from a defeated army.
We definitely did not want to be classed as stragglers. There
was no possibility at that point of adopting aggressive guerrilla

tactics, but when we learned all we needed to about the terrain, we would go on the offensive and take control of the island.

In this connection, Kozuka was very important to me. I had not told him my special mission, but he seemed to sense something and was always cooperative. He never complained, nor did he once look resentful. He was quick to make decisions, and there was a positive air about him. Whenever I watched him in action, I remembered the saying about big things coming in small packages.

Akatsu finally deserted in September, 1949, four years after the four of us had come together.

I had thought this would happen some day. Kozuka, too, just shrugged and said, "This kind of life was too much for him from the beginning."

Akatsu had disappeared three times previously; each time Shimada had found him and brought him back. The first time he left, we later saw a little fire burning at night a long way off. It was deep in the mountains, and we knew it could be no one but Akatsu, so Shimada went and got him.

The second time was in the middle of the rainy season. Shimada showed me where he had lost sight of the man, and I figured out the direction in which he must have gone. Shimada, taking a pup tent with him, went off to search and six days later came back with Akatsu.

I was able to guess where he had gone because I knew where on the island he might find food in any given season. Shimada found Akatsu almost exactly at the point I had predicted.

There was a reason why it was always Shimada who went to look for Akatsu when he ran away, and this was that Akatsu always got lost when he and Shimada were out somewhere together.

The four of us had paired off, Kozuka with me and Akatsu with Shimada. The twosomes took turns doing various tasks. When something had to be done that could not be done by two men alone, we all joined forces. In hunting, for example, three men would go out, while the fourth stood guard at the encampment. Most of the time, however, we moved in pairs. When the four of us were together, I kept a close enough watch on Akatsu so that he never once fell by the wayside. Shimada, unfortunately, was not that careful.

I felt some responsibility for Akatsu's desertion. From watching his everyday actions and listening to what he said, I concluded that he would not last very long. When I worked on plans and strategy for our future movements, therefore, I discussed them only with Shimada and Kozuka and kept them secret from Akatsu. I did not even tell him where the ammunition was hidden. I remember once whispering in Kozuka's ear, "I'm taking Akatsu out an on errand with me. While we're gone, transfer the ammunition to a different place. I placed a marker on the trunk of a palm tree about thirty yards away, so you can see where to put it."

If Akatsu deserted and surrendered, he would certainly be forced or persuaded to give the enemy information about the rest of us. This prospect seriously affected my attitude. We were after all at war with a fearsome enemy, and nothing could have been more infuriating to me than the idea that one of our group might betray the others. Suspecting that Akatsu might defect, I took the precautions that seemed necessary, but this may have had the effect of making him feel left out.

When Akatsu disappeared the fourth time, Shimada started to go look for him, but this time Kozuka and I argued that it was a waste of effort. We did this with the knowledge that Akatsu would eventually tell the enemy everything he knew about our group.

We expected that the enemy would launch an attack based

on the information Akatsu supplied, but we were confident now that if we made advance preparation, we would not be captured.

Beyond that, there was a possibility that Akatsu on his own might not survive long enough to be taken by the enemy. While he was with us, he was never sick once, largely because we were always thinking of his health and always protecting him. On the three previous occasions when he had gone away, he had come back in a depleted physical condition. I thought to myself that if we were in the dry season, he might have a chance, but now, in the rainy season, I doubted whether he would have the stamina to survive. I predicted that he would die somewhere in the mountains, wet, shivering and emaciated.

But then Akatsu must also have been aware of what he was up against. If that was the case, his departure must mean that he was really fed up. Unlike me, he had no assignment, no objective, and the struggle to keep alive here in the mountains may well have come to seem pointless to him.

Shimada went off in the rain to look for him anyway, but came back a week later alone and completely worn out. My feeling was one of relief. I did not believe in chasing after a defector to begin with, and by this time I had come to regard Akatsu's departure as good riddance.

Shimada asked anxiously, "Do you suppose he'll lead the enemy to us?"

"Probably," replied Kozuka, in a tone indicating that he thought it only to be expected. I was convinced then that Kozuka had also expected Akatsu to desert sooner or later.

The place where Akatsu had disappeared was toward the western end of our circuit, deep in the forest near Snake Mountain Abutment. We were later astonished to find that he surrendered at Looc, toward the eastern end of the island —and not until six months afterward. I was amazed and a little chagrined that his luck had held out that long.

About ten months after Akatsu's departure, and only a few
days after the end of the rainy season in 1950, we found a note
saying, "When I surrendered, the Philippine troops greeted
me as a friend." The note was written in Akatsu's hand. Shortly
afterward we spotted a light aircraft circling slowly in the
sky above Vigo. Taking this to mean that the enemy was
about to start looking for us, we moved over to the other side
of the island.

The next day we heard a loudspeaker that seemed to be
somewhat north of Wakayama Point. The voice said: "Yesterday we dropped leaflets from an airplane. You have three
days, that is, seventy-two hours, in which to surrender. In the
event that you do not surrender in that time, we will probably
have no alternative but to send a task force after you."

The voice spoke in Japanese, with no trace of a foreign
accent, but the choice of words sounded American. Japanese
do not speak of three days as "seventy-two hours," and the
whole announcement impressed us as being a translation
from some foreign tongue. For them to ask us in strange-
sounding Japanese to surrender was still more proof that the
war had not ended.

I had come to this island on the direct orders of the division
commander. If the war were really over, there ought to be
another order from the division commander releasing me from
my duties. I did not believe that the division commander would
forget orders that he had issued to his men.

Supposing he had forgotten. The orders would still have
been on record at division headquarters. Certainly somebody
would have seen to it that the commander's outstanding orders
were properly rescinded.

Three days later, we spotted the expected task force from a
distance of about 150 yards.

Kozuka whispered, "That idiot Akatsu has really brought
the Americans. Let's try to get a good look at them!"

The enemy troops were on a road that runs through a forest of palms east of the Agcawayan River and inland from Brol. They were not Americans but Filipino soldiers, and there were only about five or six of them, carrying a loudspeaker with them. In front was a man in a white hiking hat, walking somewhat nervously.

"That's Akatsu, isn't it?" whispered Kozuka. We squinted, but we could not see his face well enough to tell. After the task force moved on, we persuaded ourselves that it had indeed been Akatsu, now working for the enemy.

After this encounter, Kozuka said, "They couldn't take us prisoner with a force of fifty or even a hundred men. We know this island better than anybody else in the world!"

The main thing that bothered me was the fear that the enemy might try using gas. This would do us in immediately, because we had no gas masks. As an emergency measure, I told the others to keep a towel tied to their canteen straps and in the event of an attack to soak the towel in water and hold it over their faces. I also warned them to keep an eye on the direction of the wind, because the wind would blow the gas in. We did not abandon our makeshift gas masks for six months.

THREE SOLDIERS AT WAR

After Akatsu surrendered, we were able to take a more positive course of action. We speeded up the trips around our circuit of campsites, which we began to regard as inspection tours of the area under our "occupation." When we encountered the enemy, we fired without hesitation. After all, the enemy must have learned from Akatsu when and where they could expect to find us. We considered people dressed as islanders to be enemy troops in disguise or enemy spies. The proof that they were was that whenever we fired on one of them, a search party arrived shortly afterward.

The number of enemy troops increased every time they came, and it looked as though they were trying to surround us and then kill us. By and by, I began to wonder if they were not eventually going to launch an all-island campaign.

To search all the hills and valleys in the central area at one time, however, would require at least one or two battalions, and it seemed unlikely that they would send such a large force just to capture three men. My guess was that they would never send more than fifty or a hundred troops. We were confident that we could cut our way through a force no larger than that. We had the advantage of knowing central Lubang like the backs of our hands. In fact, the largest force we ever saw numbered no more than one hundred; usually there were only about fifty.

When we fled into the jungle, the large trees became our

94

protectors. Sometimes the enemy troops would continue firing
for some time at the trees we were hiding behind, but this did
them no good. As they grew more and more frustrated, they
aimed less carefully and wasted still more ammunition. That
was exactly what we wanted them to do. We were only three
men, but we were making a force of fifty look silly. That is the
kind of warfare I had been taught at Futamata.

I told Shimada and Kozuka about my orders from the division commander.

Kozuka immediately said, "Lieutenant, I'll stay with you to
the end, even if it takes ten years."

Shimada spoke even more enthusiastically. "The three of us
ought to secure this whole island before our troops land
again."

The two of them usually addressed me as "Lieutenant" or
"Commander," but there was no real distinction of rank among
us. I was an officer, Shimada a corporal, and Kozuka a
private first class, but we talked as equals, each of us having
an equal say in the laying of plans. We took turns hunting and
cooking.

I hid my sword in the trunk of a dead tree not far from
Kumano Point. This left me armed just like the other two, with
a rifle and a bayonet. The three of us were comrades, fighting
for the same goal, and we had a good deal in common. None
of us drank, all of us had healthy teeth, and, in general, we were
all healthy. Although Shimada was somewhat larger than the
other two of us, we were all small enough to move about with
the speed required for guerrilla tactics.

I do not mean that we had no quarrels. Far from it! There
were times when we were frothing at the mouth and taking
pokes at each other.

In our heads we carried a "food-distribution map" of
Lubang. From the weather and from experience, we could tell
which part of the island we should go to to find ripe bananas or

a relatively large number of cows. It often happened, however, that when we arrived at the spot indicated by our food
map, there was not as much food as we had hoped, and a clash
of opinions would ensue.

"Let's go farther inland."

"No, let's rest here for a day."

"Nonsense! Why do you want to do that?"

"Why shouldn't I?"

"That's about enough back talk out of you!"

"Who do you think you are, ordering me around?"

Once this started, it went on until somebody gave in.
Shimada and Kozuka sometimes came to blows, and there
was an occasional split lip or sore arm. When they went at it,
I usually mediated, but sometimes I just sat still and let them
fight it out by themselves. When that happened, there was
nothing they could do but fight tooth and nail until one or
the other surrendered unconditionally. This struck me as a
good thing, because it gave them a chance to test their physical
strength and find out how far their bodies would go along with
their convictions. In the long run, the occasional fights brought
us closer together.

One time I came to blows with Shimada. We were talking
about Akatsu's defection, and Shimada took a sympathetic
view toward Akatsu. I, for my part, had no sympathy at all
for a soldier who had deserted before my very eyes. Before very
long a fistfight started, and we rolled down the hill pounding
each other.

Often when we were walking at the foot of the mountains
near a village, we found waste paper and worn-out clothing.
The latter was most welcome, because we were always running
out of rags to polish our rifles with. These days, too, the islanders who came into the mountains to cut trees often left

uneaten rice in their pots. These traces of waste meant to us that living conditions on the island had improved somewhat. At the time when Akatsu left, you could have walked over the whole island without finding a scrap of waste paper.

One night Shimada, who had gone out on patrol, came back and said, somewhat excitedly, "Lieutenant, don't make any noise, but come with me."

We were near the Tilik area. I followed him silently up a small hill that had been left bald by the recent harvesting of rice. When we reached the top, I suppressed a gasp. Electric lights were shining in Tilik! It was the first time since I had been on Lubang that I had seen electric lights.

The three of us sat down on the hill and stared at the town.

"When do you suppose they got generators?"

"Let's try going a little closer."

"No! They've never had electricity before. Let them enjoy it for a while."

It had been six years since I had seen electric lights, but the sight of them did not make me the slightest bit homesick. That surprised even me. I had become so accustomed to having no lights at night that Tilik just looked like a different world from the one I was living in.

The ships coming into Tilik changed too. At first there had been small vessels that looked for all the world like *pokkuri*, the high-base wooden clogs once worn by Japanese geisha. We called them *pokkuri* boats. Now these had given way to large white ocean liners, some of which played music over their loudspeakers when they were anchored in Tilik. They usually played popular Filipino songs, but sometimes we heard a Japanese melody. The sound floated all the way up to the little bald hill where we first saw the lights of Tilik.

We could also see the lighthouse at Cabra, a neighboring island. The sight of something outside Lubang affected me not at all, and I wondered whether I had lost my ability to feel.

In the rainy season neither the search parties nor the islanders came to the mountains. We could relax and stay in one place. We built a little shelter with a roof made of palm leaves. Sometimes we would sit here all day. If you are in one place for a long time, you grow accustomed to the sounds around you. When we were on the move, the slightest sound set us on edge, but when we were in the same place for a long time, we began to recognize this sound as the crackling of twigs in the wind and that sound as rising water in the nearby valley, and so on. We learned to distinguish the birds that lived only in particular localities.

When we were like this, the usual tension left us, and we talked about old times back in Japan. We probably knew more about each other's family background and childhood than most of our relatives knew.

Once in a while Shimada would say softly, "I wonder whether it was a boy or a girl."

When he had left home, he and his wife were expecting their second child. The first, a girl, had not yet started primary school. One time when Shimada was talking about her, he sighed and said, "I guess she must be about the age to like boys now." Then he just stared at his feet as the rain fell on outside.

Shimada particularly liked to talk about the *bon*-festival dances in his hometown. Whenever he started on this subject, his face would light up, and his voice become animated. Every once in a while he would break out into the song they sang in his town for the festival

> The only ones who aren't dancing tonight
> Are the old stone Buddha and me.

He told us about the wooden stage they used to build for the dances and how the young men would strut about on it in their summer kimonos. As the song went on and on to the steady beating of drums, the men and women would dance around in a circle. The traditional words of the song would gradually be replaced by bawdy variations, until, as dawn approached, the young men would begin to sidle up to the girls.

"You must have danced at the *bon* festival, Lieutenant," Shimada once said.

But I shook my head. I did not know the song Shimada sang, and I had never been to a *bon* festival. Neither had Kozuka. All we could do was listen.

"The *bon* festival is the happiest time of the year," Shimada would say, often repeating himself. I like to remember him this way, because it was at times like these that I was most strongly impressed with his essential goodness.

Sometimes we cut each other's hair with some little scissors I had improvised. I cut Shimada's, Shimada cut Kozuka's, and Kozuka cut mine. If two of us cut each other's, eventually one of the two would have to cut the third one's hair, and that would not have been fair. It took about forty minutes per haircut, and if one person cut two others', he would be working nearly an hour and a half, whereas one of the others would not have worked at all.

In February, 1952, a light aircraft from the Philippine Air Force circled over the island. We heard the sound of a loud-speaker, but I could not make out what it was saying because of the noise of the engine. Kozuka, who had good ears, said, "They seem to be calling our names." After he said that, that is what it sounded like to me too. The airplane dropped some leaflets and left.

We picked up the leaflets later, and among them was a letter from my oldest brother, Toshio. The letter started, "I am entrusting this letter to Lieutenant Colonel Jimbo, who is going to the Philippine Islands on the invitation of Madame Roxas." It went on to say that the war had ended, that my parents were both well and that my brothers were all out of the army.

There were also letters from Kozuka's and Shimada's families, together with family photographs.

My reaction was that the Yankees had outdone themselves this time. I wondered how on earth they had obtained the photographs. That there was something fishy about the whole thing was beyond doubt, but I could not figure out exactly how the trick had been carried out. The photograph Shimada received showed his wife and two children. If the photograph was genuine, the second child was a girl, but we had some doubts about this.

"It's supposed to be a photograph of my immediate family," remarked Shimada, "but that man on the left is not in my immediate family. He's only a relative. I think this is just another enemy hoax."

I heard after I returned to Japan that when Lieutenant Colonel Nobuhiko Jimbo was in the Philippines during the war, he saved the life of Manuel Roxas, who became president after the war. Roxas died in 1948, and later his widow invited Lieutenant Colonel Jimbo to the Philippines for a visit. He had indeed brought the letters, but we could not believe it at the time.

About a month later, we heard another loudspeaker. A man's voice said, "I was staying at the Manila Hotel, when I heard that you were still on this island. I came to talk with you. I am Yutaka Tsuji of the *Asahi Newspaper*." After that the man kept repeating that he was Japanese, and then he sang something that sounded like a Japanese war song.

"They're at it again," I commented.

Shimada replied, "It's a nuisance. Let's move somewhere else."

Thinking that the man with the loudspeaker might have left something behind, we looked around and found a Japanese newspaper—the first one we had seen for seven years.

In the current topics section, there was a story in bold type saying, "Lieutenant Colonel Jimbo has gone to the Philippines to persuade the Philippine government to cancel its punitive missions against the Japanese soldiers on Lubang." This article had been circled in red.

We read the rest of the newspaper page by page and came to the conclusion that the enemy had devised some means to insert this article into an otherwise genuine Japanese newspaper. The talk about "punitive missions" proved, after all, that the war was still going on.

I told the other two that the newspaper was "poisoned candy." It looked good, but it was deadly.

The daily schedule of radio broadcasts in the paper disturbed me a little. It seemed to me that there were far too many light entertainment programs. I knew, however, that in America there were commercial radio stations, and I decided that there must now be commercial stations in Japan. When I left the country, there was only the government-operated network, but there might be commercial stations now. If there were, it stood to reason that they would have to present a good deal of light entertainment in order to attract advertisers.

Kozuka said, "I don't think there *is* any reporter named Yutaka Tsuji. I think they're just trying to be slick, using the name of the *Asahi Newspaper* and all that stuff."

In June, 1953, Shimada was wounded badly in the leg. This happened on the south shore between Gontin and Binacas.

We considered this a part of our territory. Since islanders rarely came near it, we were surprised one day to find that a group of fifteen or sixteen fishermen had made camp there. The rainy season was approaching, and we could not risk having people this near our hiding place. I said, "Let's clear them out right now. The sooner, the better!"

Before dawn, the fishermen built a fire and gathered around it to warm themselves. From a nearby grove, Shimada and Kozuka fired some shots in their direction. They scattered, but one of them seized a gun and hid behind a boulder. We started out on a roundabout path that would bring us out behind him. We did not know that in the meanwhile another of the fishermen, armed with a carbine, had returned to the beach. Our sudden appearance startled him, and he fired two blind shots at us before fleeing.

One of the shots hit the ring finger of my right hand; the other went through Shimada's right leg. He dropped to his knees and remained motionless. I hurriedly pulled him up and carried him on my back into the forest, while Kozuka covered our rear.

The bullet had entered the inner side of the knee and gone through slantwise. I took off my loincloth and made a tourniquet above the wound.

Carbine bullets are small, and it appeared that there was no damage to the bone. There was no dirt in the wound either, so I did not think there was any danger of tetanus. I sealed the wound with cow fat and made a splint from the knee to the ankle. Shimada gritted his teeth in pain, sweat pouring from his forehead.

After that, I boiled water and bathed the wound every day. I sucked on and around the opening to bring the blood, and then I applied fresh cow fat. We had no medicine of any kind. An extra loincloth and the cow fat were the only medicaments available.

While I was trying to be doctor to Shimada, Kozuka took charge of standing guard and procuring food. Shimada could not move, and I had to nurse him, even carrying away his waste. I was grateful that the rainy season had set in. Otherwise, it would have been perilous to remain in the same place long enough for Shimada's wound to heal.

After about forty days, there was a thin layer of skin over the wound. Although there was no more danger of festering, it was a serious wound, and there was a distinct possibility that Shimada would be crippled. I told him to try moving his leg at the knee. Slowly he did so, bending his ankle at the same time. Kozuka and I were immensely relieved.

But Shimada's big toe was rigid, making it impossible for him to get around very fast. He looked depressed.

One day when Kozuka and I returned from hunting, we found Shimada lying on his stomach, preparing to shoot at something we could not see. We quickly dropped to the ground, and I asked in a low voice what was up. He glanced back and then, holding his gun, turned over on his back. His face was flushed.

"After you left," he said, "I heard voices from the direction of the shore. I think about seven or eight of the islanders must have come pretty close to here. I was going to kill them if I could, but frankly I thought I'd had it."

I was afraid that Shimada might develop some side ailment, but he grew stronger by the day. His smile came back, and by the end of October he was able to walk about with his gun on his shoulder, although he still limped. He apologized any number of times for the trouble he had caused.

I was feeling very happy about his recovery, but around the end of the year, he seemed to lose spirit. He looked gloomy a good deal of the time and began to reminisce about his father and his grandfather. His tone was quiet and somehow sad.

Shimada lacked the vitality he had had before. I remembered what I had heard from an old soldier a long time ago: "A light wound makes you braver, but a serious wound can make you lose your nerve." Maybe that was what had happened to Shimada. In the evening, when he sat looking at the picture of his wife and children that had been dropped with the leaflets, I sensed that the weight of nearly forty years rested heavily on his shoulders. He had gotten much grayer.

He talked to himself a good deal now. One day when I asked him what he had said, he just shook his head and replied, "Oh, nothing."

Not many days later, I found him staring blankly at the photograph. Thinking I would cheer him up, I walked up behind him, but before I spoke, I heard him say quietly, "Ten years. Ten whole years."

I slipped silently back to where I had been, but with an awful premonition. Back when he was his normal self, he had taken difficulties lightly.

"Don't worry," he had always said, "It'll all be back in our hands tomorrow."

That was his way of saying that everything would be all right tomorrow. He had bucked Kozuka and me up any number of times with that phrase. Now it was different, and I was afraid.

My fears came true several months later.

The beach at Gontin was unlucky for Shimada. On May 7, 1954, he was killed at a spot only about half a mile from the place where he had been wounded in the leg.

After he recovered enough from the leg wound to walk, we moved to a place near Wakayama Point, but catching sight of a search party, we started down toward the south shore. Unfortunately, another search party was waiting for us there. There were about thirty-five of them, clustered on the beach like a flock of seagulls, only about eight hundred yards away. I thought the best thing to do was open fire on them. If we fired ten shots, we would get a few of them. Then we should be able to get away before they recovered from their shock.

But after I thought a moment, I remembered that Shimada's leg might not be strong enough for this. As in the case of Akatsu, we would have to adapt our movements to the weakest of the three; Shimada at this point was the weakest. I still thought we could probably make it, but there was a tinge of doubt, and besides, I did not want us to use any more ammunition than we absolutely had to.

Kozuka was preparing to fire, and I took aim too, but then I changed my mind.

"Don't shoot," I said. "We can always kill some of them whenever we want to. Let's let them live a little longer."

Calling off the attack, we went back into the woods. It looked peaceful enough in the ravine, but we had to be careful. The search party might come inland from the shore.

We were of three different opinions as to what we should do next. Kozuka wanted to cross the mountains and shift toward the opposite shore in one move. Out of consideration for Shimada's leg, I argued that we should go around the mountains, trying to stay at about the same level all the way. This would take longer but would involve less physical strain.

Kozuka turned to Shimada and asked, "What do you want to do?"

Shimada replied sheepishly, "I have so much trouble moving around that I would like to dig in here."

Kozuka was furious. "Your leg's well, isn't it?" he shouted. "We'd be crazy to stay here. Akatsu knows this place. The search party is bound to come sooner or later. Are you with us or against us, Shimada? If you're against us, I've got another idea about what to do!"

Kozuka stuck the muzzle of his rifle against Shimada's chest. Underneath his visor, his eyes were fiery with rage. I pushed the rifle aside and said, "Calm down, Kozuka. It wouldn't be very smart to drag him off if he isn't sure of his leg. Let's do as he says and hide here for a while."

We stayed.

There was a fruit called *nanka* that grew in abundance in

this area, and the next morning Kozuka and I picked a large
bunch of them. We decided to slice them and put them out
to dry. There was a recess midway up the cliff by the valley;
the upper slope was not visible from the bottom of the valley.
We found a fallen tree in a sunny place on this slope and
lined the sliced *nanka* up along the trunk. Then Kozuka and I
returned across the valley to our camp and lay down to take a
nap, leaving Shimada to stand watch. When we awoke, we
found that Shimada had moved the *nanka* down into the valley,
because the fallen tree trunk was now in the shade.

"That's not good," mumbled Kozuka.

If anyone saw the *nanka*, he would know we were hiding
nearby. I was worried about this too, but I was more worried
about the seach party on the shore. The day before, they had
moved off toward Two House Point. Now I was afraid they
might come back. I decided we should eat while it was still
light and then, taking our food with us, move back over
toward the shore to see what was going on. I left the *nanka*
where they were and started cooking. By doing so I caused
Shimada's death.

While I was cooking, I glanced down in the valley and caught
sight of some slight movement. I grabbed my rifle. A man who
looked like an islander was climbing down into the valley,
only about twenty-five yards away. He had obviously spotted
the *nanka*. I fired two quick shots.

Whether the shots found their mark or not, I do not know.
The man screamed and threw himself behind a rock. I fell to
the ground, Kozuka hid behind a large tree trunk about three
yards away, and we prepared to fire another round.

But Shimada continued to stand by a tree some yards away.
His gun was aimed, but he had not fired a shot. This was
peculiar, because he was the fastest shot of us all. He could
fire five times while I was firing twice. What bothered me
more was that he was still standing.

Under normal circumstances, I would have shouted, "Get down, you fool!" But for some reason, on that one occasion I had no voice. I did not know where the enemy was, but if the man I had seen was their guide, they were somewhere nearby. If they had come up from the shore through the valley, they might be in a place where they could see us clearly.

A shot rang out in the valley, and Shimada fell forward head first. He did not move. He was killed instantly. The enemy was not in the valley, as I had thought, but on the slope across the river. That meant Kozuka and I were exposed, so we scrambled up the bank behind us. We held onto our guns, but left everything else behind—tools, ammunition pack, bolo knives, everything.

According to a newspaper that a later search party left behind, Shimada was hit between the eyebrows. The newspaper also said that what we had taken for a search party was a Philippine Army mountain unit practicing for attacks on the Huks. This did not alter the hatred Kozuka and I felt for the people who had shot Shimada.

We always wondered why Shimada had remained standing without firing a shot. I suspected that the enemy troops might have been displaying a Japanese flag, and that the sight of it might have made Shimada hesitate for that one fateful moment. Perhaps he saw the flag and thought that at last troops had arrived to reestablish contact with us. To display the enemy's flag would have been a standard ploy for a guerrilla unit.

However that may be, we had made several mistakes. The first was to hide in that valley, the second was to move the *nanka* down into the valley, and the third was to leave them there. It had been a mistake for Shimada to remain standing and a mistake for me not to call to him to get down.

Why had my voice deserted me? The only explanation I can think of is that unless we were fighting with each other, the three of us never talked in a loud voice. I never even gave orders in a loud voice. Conceivably habit could have prevented me from crying out immediately. But did that really hold water? Shouldn't I have been able to raise my voice when I wanted to?

I cursed myself for not having done so, but Kozuka said, "It was Shimada who wanted to stay there in the first place. It may sound callous, but we have to get used to the fact that he's dead. It worries me to see you go on blaming yourself for what happened."

About ten days after Shimada died, a Philippine Air Force plane trailing a streamer behind it passed over several times. It dropped leaflets, and a loudspeaker kept saying, "Onoda, Kozuka, the war has ended."

This infuriated us. We wanted to scream out to the obnoxious Americans to stop threatening and cajoling us. We wanted to tell them that if they did not stop treating us like scared rabbits, we would get back at them someday, one way or another.

A few days after that there was a noise in the forest. I listened closely and decided it was only islanders cutting trees, but we quickly moved on to a different campsite. Afterward, I found out from a pamphlet left by a search party in 1959 that around the time in question my brother Toshio and Kozuka's younger brother Fukuji had been in Lubang looking for us.

After about two months, we went again to the valley where Shimada had been killed. I had had my fights and quarrels with Shimada, but he was a faithful friend who fought side by side with me for ten whole years. I stood there for quite a while, my hands together in prayer. Together, Kozuka and I vowed that somehow we would avenge Shimada's death.

It started to get dark, and Kozuka said, "Come on, Lieutenant, let's go."

I wiped my cheek with the back of my hand. For the first time since I came to Lubang, I was crying.

FAKED MESSAGES

One day, in a dense forest not far from the place where Shimada was killed, I found a Japanese flag on which the names of my family and some of my relatives had been written. Among the names were "Yasu" and "Noriko," which presumably stood for my oldest brother's wife Yasue and a cousin called "Nori." But if the signatures were genuine, why was the the final *e* omitted from Yasue and *ko* added to Nori? I came to the conclusion that the flag must be a fake message of some sort.

We did not believe for an instant that the war had ended. On the contrary, we expected the Japanese army to send a landing force to Lubang or at least to send secret agents to establish contact with us.

As I pondered the flag with the names of my cousin and sister-in-law written incorrectly, I had the feeling that it was trying to tell me something. I finally came to the conclusion that it was a fake message from Japanese headquarters.

My reasoning was like this. Suppose first that the Japanese army sent a spy to establish contact with me, and the Americans found out about it. The Americans would certainly reason that Japanese forces were planning to reoccupy the airfield at Lubang, because it was the only airfield in the Philippines west of Manila and would be the obvious base for an attack from the west on that city. In order to block this move, the Americans would transfer sea and air forces to Manila, thus

109

releasing pressure on Japanese troops in New Guinea, Malaya and French Indo-China. From the Japanese viewpoint, then, it made good sense to try to make the Americans think a spy was being dispatched to Lubang. Hence the flag, ostensibly intended for me, was allowed to fall into enemy hands. Now the Americans were trying to use it to entice us out of our base in the middle of Lubang. On the chance that this might happen, Japanese headquarters had taken the precaution of writing the names of my cousin and sister-in-law wrong. Since this was something that I was bound to notice, it would warn me that the whole thing was fake.

Today all this sounds ridiculous, but I had been taught at Futamata always to be on the lookout for fake messages, and it did not seem to me that my attitude was overly cautious. Indeed, I would have considered it extremely careless at the time not to question each and every character written on the flag.

I still remembered learning at Futamata about a fake message that had made it easier for Germany to overrun France in 1940. As the Germans prepared to attack France, they allowed a known Allied spy to "steal" a plan for a German aerial assault on London. The English were fooled by the plan to the extent that they hastily withdrew airplanes and antiaircraft artillery from Holland to the London area. With the English forces in Holland thus reduced, the Germans fell on that country and Belgium and then broke through the relatively weak end of the Maginot line. With in about a month they occupied Paris.

As I recalled this incident, it seemed plain to me that the Japanese flag was part of an attempt to make the enemy divert troops to Manila in the belief that Lubang was about to be reoccupied. I was excited to think that a Japanese counterattack was soon to take place.

I was not alone in regarding the flag as a fake message.

Kozuka agreed with me that it could not be anything else. I had taught Kozuka a good deal about the principles of secret warfare, and he, no less than I, had developed the habit of reading even beyond the lines between the lines. By this time he would have been a match for any graduate from Futamata.

More and more leaflets that we regarded as fake were dropped on the island, and every time they fell, we thought that the Japanese attack was drawing closer. Evidently the Japanese forces in other places were advancing to the extent that they could start harassing the enemy in the Philippines.

Whenever we found new leaflets, we were happy. We considered these "fake" messages to be in part an attempt to cheer us up. They contained a lot of information about what was going on in Japan, how our families were getting along, and sometimes there were family photographs. One leaflet that fell in 1957, for example, contained a photo captioned "Onoda-san's Family." The picture showed my parents, my older sister Chie and her children, my younger sister Keiko and several other members of my family. Everything looked genuine enough, except that a neighbor not related to me was standing over to one side. It was like the time when a person who was only a relative of Shimada's had appeared in what was supposed to be a picture of his family.

Another suspicious feature of this photo was that there was no reason why there should be a *san* after my name. "Onoda's Family" would have been proper by Japanese standards of etiquette.

There was also a photograph of "Kozuka-san's Family." Kozuka said, "How do they expect me to believe this? Why would my family be standing in front of a new house that doesn't belong to us?"

We did not know that Japanese cities had been extensively bombed, and the city of Tokyo largely reduced to ashes.

The leaflets were printed on inferior paper, presumably to

save costs. This must mean, we decided, that the leaflets were being produced in some quantity and dropped not only in Lubang but all over the Philippines. This in turn suggested that there must be many other Japanese guerrillas holding out on other islands. These leaflets were, we thought, trying to persuade them that if they made known their names and the addresses of their families, they too would receive news from the homeland, like Onoda and Kozuka on Lubang. No doubt this was the enemy's real purpose, and no doubt that is why the *san* was added to our names. In mentioning our families to other Japanese, it would be proper to use *san*.

With one set of leaflets there were envelopes with the name of the Japanese embassy in the Philippines printed on them. Once again the paper was cheap, and we concluded that the same envelopes had been dropped on Japanese troops on other islands. Each envelope contained a pencil and instructions: "Write your home address and the name of your army outfit, and we will furnish you information that will convince you. As soon as you receive this, come down from the mountains."

As to the question of how the Americans had acquired a photograph of my family, I assumed that the explanation must be something like that of the flag. It had probably been passed by a Japanese agent to the Americans or the Filipinos in the course of an attempt to foist some false information off on them. To inform me that the photograph was not to be taken seriously, the Japanese authorities had deliberately included in it a person who did not belong to my family.

I said to Kozuka, "With both sides sending all sorts of messages like this, the Japanese counterattack must be coming soon."

"Yes," he agreed, "our side isn't missing any tricks, is it?"

After I landed on Lubang at the end of 1944, I had no real knowledge of how the war was going. There was no news at all from the outside world for several years, and I did not believe the leaflets. Kozuka was in the same position as I; we both believed that it was our duty to hold out until the East Asia Co-Prosperity Sphere was firmly established. Perhaps my determination was what had brought about my appointment as a secret warfare agent in the first place. Kozuka was under no special orders like mine. He had simply been drafted into the army and sent to the Philippines. But he had been with me a long time and felt the same way I did about the situation. Neither of us doubted for a minute that there must be other Japanese soldiers like us on many of the Philippine Islands.

In 1950, just after Akatsu defected, a number of poles from Japanese army pup tents had floated up on the south shore of the island, along with fragments of army backpacks. These were blown in by the wind during the rainy season. and we took them to be debris from a passing Japanese troop transport. The presence of a troop transport in this region in turn suggested that the main fighting was now centered in Indo-China.

Five years later it stood to reason that the front had been extended to Java or Sumatra, and we judged that a joint air, sea and land campaign must be going on all over the area to the south.

We were impressed by the continued enemy patrol activity in our area. Around 1950 lighthouses went into operation on Cabra and on the northwest end of Mindoro; from then on two patrol planes covered the area every day. And the number of fighter planes continually increased. At first there had been only two or three a day, but now there were sometimes dozens.

What convinced us most of the presence of other Japanese troops in the islands was the occasional dropping of bombs in the valley near Vigo. After it was all over, I learned that Lubang had become a practice target for Philippine Air Force training planes, but at the time I could only speculate as to the reason for the bombs. I came to the conclusion that the enemy believed we were trying to bring in Japanese guerrilla units from other islands. The bombs were being dropped to prevent this.

Around May, 1954, a voice speaking over a loudspeaker said, "I am Katsuo Sato, former chief of staff of the Naval Air Force. I would like to meet you in Looc." It seemed to us ridiculous that a naval officer would come looking for us when we were both in the army.

In sum, the various leaflets and "fake" messages that reached us on Lubang, far from convincing us that the war was over, persuaded us that Japanese troops would soon be landing on the island. Thinking that any advance Japanese agent would certainly come ashore on the south coast, we were trying to "secure" that area. We believed that if, when this agent arrived, we were unable to give him all the information he needed about the island, we would be severely reprimanded, and rightly so.

The south shore would be the best place for Japanese troops to land. They could anchor their boats on the reefs and walk through sixty or seventy yards of shallow water to the beach, from which they could immediately run into the mountains. If they were to say, for example, that they wanted to proceed from this point to the airfield within two days, we were prepared to guide them in the specified time along a route where they would not encounter enemy troops.

We tried, by firing occasional warning shots, to keep islanders out of the south coast area, and we spent a good deal of time working out the safe route to the airfield. I did not know until much later that because of our tactics, the Filipinos had decided to fire on us at sight.

In the spring of 1958, the Philippine Air Force began building a radar base on the mountain we knew as Five Hundred. Before actual construction began, the air force hired a large number of islanders to construct a motor road leading up to the base. One day when we went out to see how the road was coming along, we were surprised by the sound of an explosion near the top of the mountain. We looked at each other in surprise.

Kozuka said, "Looks like they're starting to build in earnest."

I replied, "Let's wait until dark and take a look around up there."

We sat down on the side of the hill and waited for sunset, which would be in about thirty minutes. I had my back to the ridge, and Kozuka, who was sitting beside me in such a position that he could keep an eye on the ridge, was talking to me in a low voice.

Suddenly he gasped, "Uh!" I whirled around and fired toward the top of the ridge. There was a cry from that direction, as somebody fell over on the other side of the ridge, We hurried down the hill into the forest.

Not long after that the large search party of 1959 arrived from Japan to look for us.

"The Americans seem to be starting another one of their fake rescue operations," I said.

"What a nuisance!" growled Kozuka. "Let's move somewhere where it's quiet."

We shifted to an area toward the south where we could not hear the loudspeakers, from which, I found out later, the search party had repeated over and over again: "Lieutenant Onoda! Private First Class Kozuka! We have come from Japan to look for you. The war has ended. Please talk with us and come back to Japan with us."

They also played the Japanese national anthem and a lot of Japanese folk songs and popular songs. The search party went around the whole island, camping out at night. Every time they came near us, we went farther into the jungle.

We were sure in our own minds that these people were

the hill, his shoulders drooping. After I saw him safely out of sight, I slipped back into the jungle.

When I returned to Japan, I learned that it really had been my brother.

"When I heard the voice go off at the end of the song," I explained, "I was convinced it was an impersonator."

With a sad look on his face, my brother said, "While I was singing, I began thinking that this was my last day on Lubang, and I choked up . . . . So you did hear me, after all."

The search party left behind newspapers and magazines. Most of them were recent, and a lot of them contained articles about the crown prince's marriage. The newspapers, which covered a period of about four months, made a stack nearly two feet high. We thought they were reprints of real Japanese newspapers doctored up by the American secret service in such a way as to eliminate any news the Americans did not want us to see. This was all we could think so long as we believed that the Greater East Asia War was still going on.

And in a way the newspapers confirmed that the war was still going on, because they told a lot about life in Japan. If Japan had really lost the war, there should not *be* any life in Japan. Everybody should be dead.

When I arrived in the Philippines in 1944, the war was going badly for Japan, and in the homeland the phrase *ichioku gyokusai* ("one hundred million souls dying for honor") was on everybody's lips. This phrase meant literally that the population of Japan would die to a man before surrendering. I took this at face value, as I am sure many other young Japanese men my age did.

I sincerely believed that Japan would not surrender so long as one Japanese remained alive. Conversely, if one Japanese were left alive, Japan could not have surrendered.

After all, this is what we Japanese had all vowed to each other. We had sworn the we would resist the American and English devils until the last single one of us was dead. If necessary, the women and children would resist with bamboo sticks, trying to kill as many enemy troops as they could before being killed themselves. The wartime newspapers all played this idea up in the strongest possible language. "Struggle to the End!" "The Empire Must Be Protected at Any Cost!" "One Hundred Million Dying for the Cause." I was virtually brought up on this kind of talk.

When I became a soldier, I accepted my country's goals. I vowed that I would do anything within my power to achieve those goals. I did not, it is true, come forward and volunteer for military service, but having been born male and Japanese, I considered it my sacred duty, once I had passed the army physical examination, to become a soldier and fight for Japan.

After I entered the army, I became a candidate in officers' training school. When my brother Tadao came to see me there, he asked me whether I was prepared to die for my country. I told him I was. At that time, I renewed my oath to myself that I would give my all. It was a solemn oath, and I was resolved to carry it out.

By 1959 I had been in Lubang for fifteen years, and the only real news I had received from Japan during that time was the newspaper left by Yutaka Tsuji, who claimed to be a reporter from the *Asahi Newspaper*. I was not even sure that this news was genuine.

In short, for fifteen years, I had been outside the flow of time. All I could be sure of was what had been true in late 1944 and what I had sworn at that time to do. I had kept my vow rigidly during those fifteen years.

Reading the 1959 newspapers in this same frame of mind, the first thought I had was, "Japan is safe, after all. Safe and still fighting!"

The newspapers offered any amount of proof. Wasn't the whole country wildly celebrating the crown prince's marriage? Didn't the pictures show a lavish wedding parade through the streets of Tokyo, with thousands of cheering Japanese lined up along the way? There was nothing here about one hundred million people dying. Japan was obviously thriving and prosperous.

Who said we had lost the war? The newspapers proved this was wrong. If we had lost, our countrymen would all be dead; there would be no more Japan, let alone Japanese newspapers.

Kozuka agreed with me completely. As we were reading the papers, he looked up and remarked, "Life in the home islands seems to be a lot better than it was when we left, doesn't it? Look at the ads. There seems to be plenty of everything. I'm glad, aren't you? I makes me feel it has been worthwhile holding out the way we have."

How could we even dream that Japan's cities had been leveled, that Japan's ships had nearly all been sunk, or that an exhausted and depleted Japan had indeed surrendered? As to the details of the defeat, such as the invasion of Manchukuo by the Soviet Union or the dropping of the atomic bomb on Hiroshima, the newspapers of 1959 gave not an inkling.

We read the newspapers through and through, right down to the little three-line want ads. As a matter of fact, the want ads were particularly interesting, because they indicated what kind of work people were seeking and what kind of people were being sought.

But time had stopped for us in 1944, and as we read, we kept finding items that we could not understand at all. We were particularly puzzled by articles on foreign relations and military affairs. Sometimes after we had read them several times, they still meant nothing.

It was difficult to tell, for example, which countries were now on Japan's side and which were not. Putting together what we read in the newspapers and the bits and pieces of information (or misinformation) we had gleaned from leaflets and the like, we formed a total picture of Japan and the war situation in 1959.

We knew that the Great Japanese Empire had become a democratic Japan. We did not know when or how, but clearly there was now a democratic government, and the military organization had been reformed. It also appeared as though Japan was now engaged in cultural and economic relations with a large number of foreign countries.

The Japanese government was still working for the establishment of the Greater East Asia Co-Prosperity Sphere, and the new army was still engaged in military conflict with America. The new army seemed to be a modernized version of the old army, and we supposed that it must have assumed responsibility for the defense of East Asia as a whole, China included.

China was now a communist country under the leadership of Mao Tse-tung: there seemed little doubt but that Mao had come to power with the support of Japan. No doubt he was now cooperating with Japan to implement the co-prosperity sphere. Although there was nothing in the newpapers about this, it was only logical that the American secret service would have eliminated any mention of it in preparing the newspapers for us.

We calculated that Japan would have found it advantageous to set Mao Tse-tung up as the leader of the New China, because this would make the vast sums of money held by wealthy Chinese financiers available to Japan. We assumed that to secure Japan's support, Mao had agreed to drive the Americans and English out of China and to cooperate with the new Japanese army.

Fundamentally, Japan and China were working for the same goal. It seemed only natural that they would have formed an alliance. We started speaking of this as the "East Asia Co-Prosperity League," and we assumed that Manchukuo was also an active member, contributing materially in the field of arms manufacture.

Kozuka asked, "Do you suppose those are the only three countries in the league?"

"No," I answered. "I would think that the eastern part of Siberia had by now broken away from the Soviet Union and joined the league."

"Siberia?" he asked incredulously.

"Why not? I should think it would be only a matter of time until the White Russians in eastern Siberia would rebel against communist atheism and secede from the Soviet Union."

"Then you think there might be an independent 'Siberian Christian Republic'? Maybe you're right—it makes a good deal of sense. What about the southern regions?"

"Java and Sumatra have no doubt been liberated from Holland by now. I imagine they belong to the league too."

I remember that more than twenty of my fellow students at Futamata had been sent to Java to lead the Javanese troops there in guerrilla warfare.

"What about India?" asked Kozuka.

"I guess that it's independent from England now, and that Chandra Bose is president, or premier, or whatever the head of the country is called. I can't decide whether I think it belongs to the league or not. What do you think?"

"Well, my guess is that it's at least a friendly nation. Australia may still be holding out, but it shouldn't be too long before the Australians join us too. Anyway, that leaves us with East Siberia, Manchukuo, China, Java and Sumatra all in the league and supporting Japan in the war against America and England. The big question is when will the Philippines split off from America and join our side?"

"I think it's only a matter of time," I said confidently.

We also worked out a theory about the organization of the new Japanese military establishment. We felt that basically it could not be very different from the old. There must still be a division into army, navy and air force, and certainly there would be a secret service. We supposed also that the chain of command was the same as it had been, and that we ourselves were consequently under the command of the new organization. The new army, too, must be the source of the fake messages that were sometimes sent to Lubang. The main difference, as far as we could see, was that the conscription system had been replaced by a volunteer system.

At Futamata I had been told that to establish the East Asia Co-Prosperity Sphere, including Southeast Asia, would probably require a hundred years of warfare. A hundred-year war would wear any nation down; in Japan, where the army and the people were fighting as one, the effects would be all the more serious. If we tried to fight for a hundred years the way we were fighting in 1944, we might end up with a military victory. By that time, however, the people would be not only spiritually depleted but reduced to the depths of penury.

Because of this, I considered it likely that Japan had switched to a new system in which the soldiers fought on the military front, but the civilians only on the economic front. The expense of the war would, of course, have to be covered by taxes. The more I thought about this, the more I decided it was the most realistic policy for perfecting the co-prosperity sphere.

If the war between America and the co-prosperity league were being carried on on this basis, civilians in the two areas would be competing with each other in the economic field. The side that was winning the economic war would obviously be able to pay more taxes to its government, which would mean more money for military purposes. This government would consequently gradually acquire the military advantage.

In short, it seemed to me that the co-prosperity league,

under Japan's leadership, must still be engaged in all-out economic and military war against America, but at the same time economic affairs and military affairs were being kept separate. When Kozuka and I discussed the matter together, we always came to this conclusion, and it was only strengthened by the bits of news that we picked up on Lubang in later years. This was our conclusion, and gradually it became our creed.

"If we are right about all this," Kozuka asked, "then who are *we* fighting for?"

"For Japan and the Japanese people, of course," I replied without hesitation. "The new army must have assumed all the authority of the old army. If we are fighting for the new army, we are still fighting for the country."

Some may think it strange that even after being out of things for fifteen years I could dream up the idea of a war in which military and civilian activities were separate—a war in which Japanese and American civilians competed in the economic field while Japanese and American soldiers fought it out on the military front.

The idea did not seem very odd to me at the time, however. After all, when I was in Hankow working for the trading company and dancing my feet off at night at the dance hall, my brother Tadao was there too, fighting against the Chinese army. In those days, if one went out even as far as the suburbs of Hankow, one was in dangerous territory, and I remember hearing gunfire when I made the rounds of our suppliers in those areas. Within the city, however, the Chinese were going calmly about their business, and at the dance hall young Chinese girls from Shanghai were gaily practicing the latest dance steps with Japanese soldiers so recently back from the front that their uniforms still smelled of gunpowder. Whenever my brother came back from a military camapign, we would go out for a big dinner at one of the Chinese restaurants. In Hankow I lived alongside the Chinese and did business with them; none of us paid too much attention to the war that was going on around us. Nobody told me that there was anything unusual about all this. I took it as a matter of course.

If the search parties that came to Lubang had left us reduced-size editions of all the newpapers between 1944 and 1959, both Kozuka and I would probably have recognized that the war was over, and that we were wasting our lives. But I had been taught that the war might last a hundred years, and I had received special orders directly from a lieutenant general, who had assured me that eventually the Japanese army would come after me, no matter how long it might take. I was not able to take the 1959 Japanese newspapers at face value. I was sure from the beginning that they were part of an American deception, and I was more than ready to reject anything that did not fit in with my preconceptions. Moreover, I clearly remembered the days in Hankow when the people and the soldiers were two different things entirely.

Kozuka and I knew absolutely nothing of the postwar occupation of Japan or the San Francisco treaty. When we came across items in the newspapers that seemed inexplicable to us, we "translated" them into ideas that we could comprehend. We decided, for example, that "American bases in Japan" really meant "co-prosperity league bases in Japan," and that "Soviet rockets" were "Japanese rockets." We thought we were seeing through American attempts to deceive us by altering the original news articles.

Silly as it seems today, when we read about the Japan-U.S. Security Treaty, we decided that it must be some pact between the Japanese government and the new Japanese military establishment. The Self-Defense Force seemed to be an armed constabulary separate from the new army.

Understandably, the 1959 newspapers gave us few clues as

to how the fighting war would be decided. We could only guess that the opposing forces were now fighting it out in the Pacific, and that at some point the side with the most remaining battleships and airplanes would win out. This made us feel that the longer we could hold out on Lubang, the more advantageous it would be to our side. We were, we believed, contributing to the firm establishment of the East Asia Co-Prosperity Sphere.

In sum, working with my limited knowledge of economics and my memory of the situation in Hankow before I entered the army, I constructed an imaginary world that would fit in with the oath I had taken fifteen years earlier. During the following fifteen years, that imaginary world was unshaken either by the death of Kozuka or the arrival of numerous search parties from Japan. It stayed with me until the day Major Taniguchi gave me my final orders. In the days when I was completely alone, it seemed even more real than before. That is why I was psychologically unable to respond even when I saw members of my family and heard them calling to me. Not until I returned to Japan and looked out the window of my hotel at the streets of Tokyo did I understand that my world was no more than a figment of my imagination.

When finally I did see those thousands of cars in Tokyo, moving along the streets and the elevated expressways without a sign of war anywhere, I cursed myself. For thirty years on Lubang I had polished my rifle every day. For what? For thirty years I had thought I was doing something for my country, but now it looked as though I had just caused a lot of people a lot of trouble.

I still remember a number of items I read in the 1959 newspapers. Of them, the one that struck me most was an advertisement for a book called *Ningen Yamashita Tomobumi* ("Tomobumi Yamashita, the Man"). The ad read: "Why was it that Yamashita, who was considered the greatest

Japanese general, did not succeed in the war? Was he undercut by General Tōjō? Did he incur the wrath of the emperor? Here is the life story of the fiery militarist—a story that might be entitled *The Tragic General*."

When Kozuka and I saw that, we both assumed that it was Yankee propaganda. Neither of us believed there was a word of truth in it. General Yamashita was the commander of the Fourteenth Area Army, to which we belonged, and the idea that he had been executed for his role in the war was preposterous.

I said to Kozuka, "If the Americans feel it necessary to besmirch General Yamashita's personal character, they must really be afraid of him!"

One other article that I remember clearly was in a weekly magazine. It was about me, and the title was "Secret Mission on Lubang: What Did the Nakano School Order Lieutenant Onoda to Do?" There was an account of how Shigeichi Yamamoto, who had returned to Japan in 1955, had attended the Futamata school with me and had been ordered to conduct guerrilla warfare on Mindoro at the same time that I had received orders to go to Lubang. The article was mostly concerned, however, with the history of the Nakano School. It said that since nobody was quite sure who had issued my orders, people formerly connected with the school had started to look into the matter.

The article made me laugh. I admired the subtlety with which our secret service had composed this "fake message." There was obviously no need to explain to me the history of the Nakano School, and the secret service itself knew better than anyone else who had given me my orders. The whole thing had been trumped up to conceal a message to me. The message was, "Hang on, Onoda! We haven't forgotten you."

Such was the effect of the newspapers and magazines left by the search party of 1959. By that time, Kozuka and I had

developed so many fixed ideas that we were unable to understand anything that did not conform with them. If there
was anything that did not fit in with them we interpreted it
to mean what we wanted it to mean.

I saved all these magazines and newspapers. I intended to
submit them together with my official report when I finally
regained contact with division headquarters.

JUNGLE LIFE

If army uniforms were made out of silk serge, life would have been easier for Kozuka and me. As it was, our clothes were always rotting. During the rainy season on Lubang, it would often pour for several days in a row. Our uniforms, which we wore all the time, gave way faster to rotting than they did to wear and tear.

The trousers would rot first in the knees and the seat, then at the bottoms and in the crotch, until in the last stages, nothing was left but the backs of the legs. The jackets started at the elbows and then the back. The front part usually held together better than the rest.

To patch the holes, we had to make a needle. I found some wire netting somewhere, and we managed to straighten out a piece of the wire, sharpen it at one end, and make an eye in the other. For thread, we used the fibers of a hemplike plant that grew naturally in the forests. We would sew this vertically, horizontally and slantwise over the hole, occasionally making two layers for a quilted effect.

For the first three or four years, when we needed patches, we cut pieces of canvas off the edges of our tents, but this could be carried only so far. After that we "requisitioned" what we needed from the islanders as the opportunity presented itself.

This did not trouble our consciences. It is normal in guerrilla warfare to try to acquire guns, ammunition, food, clothing and

129

other supplies from the enemy. Since the islanders were aiding the enemy task forces that came to look for us, we considered them enemies too.

In the early years, the outfit worn by the islanders consisted of a handwoven hemp shirt and cotton knee-length shorts, neither of which was of much use to us. The islanders had thick skin, and living as they were on the plain, they required only very light clothing—too light to survive very long in the jungle thickets through which we were always moving.

The "war booty" that we valued most was the equipment that the departing American troops left behind. The islanders also prized this and kept it in a cabin that they guarded fairly closely, but occasionally we would scare them away with gunfire and make off with some of the goods, which included canteens, tents, shoes, blankets and the like. I think it was around 1951 or 1952 when we first acquired manufactured cotton cloth.

The Japanese cloth caps with flaps hanging in the back wore out in about a year. I had an officer's cap made of wool and silk, but even that gave out after about three years. From then on, I had to make my own headgear. There was a war song that started, "Even if my battle cap freezes . . ." We changed this to "Even if my battle cap rots . . ."

The clothes I had on when I came out of the jungle were some that I had remade after Kozuka's death. The front and back of my jacket were made from the lining of an islander's jumper, and the sleeves from trousers. The islander's trouser legs were not big enough around for my shoulders, but since they were too long, there was enough extra material to space out the shoulders. When I made new trousers for myself, I always reinforced the knees and the seat with leftover parts of the old trousers.

We often had to wade across streams, and to keep from wetting our clothing, we made our trousers so that they came

Cloth and clothing taken from the islanders provided the material for our clothes. When camouflage was necessary, I turned my jacket inside out and stuck small branches, sticks or leaves in loops made of fishing line for this purpose.

To make sandals, the soles were cut from tires, the "straps" from tire tubes, and the two were joined together with pegs. The upper parts of shoes were used over and over, but the soles were replaced by using the soles of islanders' sneakers. Nylon thread was best for sewing them together.

(All illustrations by Yasuo Sakaigi)

down only a little below the knee, something like riding pants. We fastened our trousers with zippers, which had come to us as part of our war booty. When we were on the move, we left the zippers open to let air in, closing them only when we slept.

We slept in our clothing, of course, and if we put the carry-all breast pockets of our jackets too high, they weighed on our chests and tended to keep us from sleeping. We therefore placed this pocket lower than the ordinary shirt pocket. It also had a zipper. Since we were always ducking under tree branches that brushed against our shoulders, we reinforced the shoulders of our jackets.

The shoes I had on when I came out were put together from real shoe leather from the tops of old shoes and rubber soles from an islander's sneakers. I had sewn these together with a thick nylon fishing line. During the early years, I had often worn straw sandles.

Around 1965 synthetic fabrics appeared on Lubang, and we gratefully "accepted" a number of articles of clothing made from them. We were also pleased by the appearance of vinyl plastic, which was useful for rain clothing and for wrapping our guns.

"They must have invented this stuff just for us," laughed Kozuka.

Our principal staple food was bananas. We cut off only the stem, sliced the bananas, skin and all, into rings about a quarter of an inch thick, and then washed them thoroughly in water. That way the green bananas lost much of their bitterness. Then we boiled them with dried meat in coconut milk. The result tasted like overcooked sweet potatoes. It was not good. But we ate this most of the time.

The rats on Lubang, which grow to a length of about eight inches, not counting the tail, eat only the pulp of the bananas, but Kozuka and I could not afford to waste the skins. At mealtime, we always said, "Let's have our feed."

Next to bananas our most important food came from cows that had been turned loose to graze. In 1945 there were about two thousand cows on the island, but their number gradually decreased to the point where it was difficult to find a fat one. Even so, three cows a year were enough to provide meat for one man.

When we could not find cows, we hunted for water buffaloes and horses. Although the water buffaloes are large and furnish a good deal of meat, it does not taste very good. Horsemeat, although tender, has a strong odor and does not taste as good as beef.

It was easiest to find cows in the rainy season. When the Lubang islanders harvest their rice, they leave about nine to twelve inches of stalk for the cows to eat. When the rice stalks are gone, the cows are turned loose at the foot of the mountains to eat grass, which grows best in the rainy season. The cows gradually work their way up the hills toward the forest, as much as to say, "Here we are. Come shoot us."

They usually grazed in herds of about fifteen. We would pick out one and fire at it from a distance of about eighty yards, aiming so that the bullet would enter beneath the backbone and go through the heart. The time to kill a cow was in the evening, after the islanders had gone home from the fields. It was nearly dark then, and if there was rain, it muffled the sound of the shot so that the farmers could not hear it.

If we hit a cow, the others would run away, frightened by the shot. Usually when we approached, the fallen cow still had life enough to move its legs. We would find a stone and smash it into the cow's forehead as hard as possible. Then we would finish it off by stabbing it in the heart with a bayonet. Having pulled it by the legs and tail to an inconspicuous spot under the trees, we cut the aorta to drain the blood.

The cow normally fell on its side, and the first step in dressing an animal was to cut off the front and hind legs on the upper

side. Then we would slash down the middle of the belly and
strip off the skin to the backbone. After cutting the meat off
in hunks, we turned the animal over and repeated the operation on the other side. Finally, we would remove the heart,
the liver, the sweetbread and other innards and put them in a
sack. It took the two of us about an hour to dismember one cow.

If we left the carcass as it was, the rain and the crows would
reduce it to a skeleton, but the remains would tell the enemy
where we were. After we cut the cow up, therefore, we moved
the carcass along a mountain road to as distant a point as
possible. This was done at night, of course. It was really heavy
work, because we had to carry all the meat on our backs at the
same time.

For the first three days, we would have fresh meat, broiled
or stewed, two times a day. Presumably because of the meat's
high calory content, as I ate, my body temperature climbed
until I felt hot to the soles of my feet. It was hard to breathe
when walking and impossible to climb a tree. My head would
always feel a little giddy.

I found that if I drank the milk of green coconuts as a
vegetable substitute when I ate meat, my temperature would
soon return to normal.

On the fourth day we piled as much meat as possible in a
pot and boiled it. By heating this up once every day and a
half or two days after that, we kept it from spoiling, and the
flavor held up for a week or ten days. While we were eating the
boiled meat, we dried what was left for future consumption.
We called this dried meat "smoked beef."

To prepare the smoked beef, we first built a framework like
a table frame. We then skewered the meat on long sticks,
placed the skewers across the framework, and built a fire
underneath. This had to be done at night in the inner reaches
of the jungle; otherwise the islanders might see the smoke or
the flame. On the first night, we would keep the fire going all

When we shot a cow, we cut the meat up, skewered it and dried it over a fire at night. During the ten days required for this, we ate boiled beef.

Piled on pieces of wood, the liver and other innards were cooked in a makeshift steamer (*left*). Small pieces of meat were boiled in a pot until the water was gone. To keep it from getting moldy, it was reheated every day.

night, so as to harden the outside of the meat a little without causing it to shrink. Afterward, we gradually increased the heat of the fire and cooked the meat about two hours a night for ten nights. By that time it was thoroughly dried. The liver and other innards, we first boiled, then dried.

From one cow, we could make about 250 slices of smoked beef. By eating only one slice apiece each day, we could make the meat last for about four months. It did not always work out this way, however, because when we were moving around a lot to keep out of the way of search parties, we allowed ourselves two slices a day.

We did not eat rice much, because it was so much trouble to hull it. In October and November, however, when the islanders harvested their rice, we usually requisitioned some of it. After pounding it, we separated it with a sieve into chaff, unpolished rice and half-polished rice. Both glutinous rice and nonglutinous rice grow on Lubang. The nonglutinous rice varies greatly in quality. We classified it into four grades, which we called "rice, 'barley' rice, 'millet' rice and fodder rice." The fodder rice was so black and the grains so small that we had trouble thinking of it as rice. When we ate rice, we made soup to go with it. This was concocted from dried meat and the leaves of papaya, eggplant or sweet potatoes, with a dash of salt and powdered pepper. Sometimes we made a gruel with rice and dried meat.

We called salt the "magic medicine." In the days when there were four of us, we had to get by on only about a quart a year. Every once in a while, whoever was cook would say, "It's cold today, so I'll put in a little of the magic medicine." And then he would put in a very tiny pinch. But even that helped the flavor a lot.

At first we had only the briny natural salt that we found on the south shore. Later, when there were only Kozuka and I, we grew more aggressive and invaded the islanders' salt flats in

Keeping rice from getting moldy was difficult, especially during the rainy season. We put it in plastic bags, then placed these in five-gallon cans sealed with plastic and oil. Since ants were a constant problem, the cans were raised off the ground on triangles of tin.

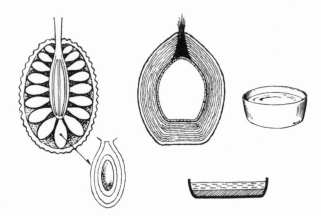

The fruit called *nanka* has a feltlike skin and a hard core surrounded by the edible portions, each of which also has a core; the taste is sweet. Coconuts provided, besides copra and milk, fibers (*seen at the top*) that we used to brush our teeth. Heating the milk settled the lees, which were boiled with water to make soup.

Looc and Tilik, but we never took more than we needed for the foreseeable future. After about 1959 we managed to obtain coffee and a few canned goods from the houses of the islanders. We called the sneak raids to obtain these valuables "stepping out for the evening."

During the thirty years on Lubang, the only thing I always had plenty of was water. The streams on the island were nearly all so clear that you could see the bottom. The only trouble was that the cows and horses that had been turned out to graze would drink water upstream and then relieve themselves in the water. For that reason, we always boiled the water before drinking it, even if it looked perfectly all right.

Having no doctor and no medicine, we were very careful to keep an eye on the condition of our health. We watched for variations in our weight by measuring the girth of our wrists. We also examined our own stool for signs of internal disorders.

I was thinnest just before Akatsu defected. I think this was partially because I was mentally upset at that time, but it was also due to a lack of sufficient nutrition. During this stage, the whites of my fingernails disappeared except for a tiny strip on my thumbs.

I examined my stool every day to see how much there was, how hard it was, and how big the pieces were. If the pieces were too big, it meant that my stomach was not functioning properly. If the stool was soft, my intestines were not absorbing enough.

If something was wrong, I had to decide for myself whether it was because of the weather, because the food I had eaten was not good, or because my body was not in good condition. Everytime something went wrong, I thought back over what I had eaten the day before, how the weather had been, and how much I had exerted myself. After I had determined the cause, I adjusted my diet and my activities accordingly.

We ate pretty much the same quantity every day, but there

was some variation, simply because some bananas are juicy and others are dry. Also, since good ripe bananas were not always available, we had to make do with green ones a great deal of the time. We tried to adjust the method of cooking to the quality of the food, then judge the effect on our insides by examining our waste. I remember deciding once not to move to a certain spot until the weather was cooler, because the last time I had spent some time there in hot weather, I had come down with diarrhea. There were other places where we could not stay long at one time because the wind chilled us too much at night. When that happened, we invariably suffered from indigestion.

When we were in a place that was too hot, our urine turned yellow, and if we overexerted ourselves, it became more red than yellow. This was a warning to take it easy for a while.

Whenever we settled down in a place, we dug a latrine, leaving the soil beside it to cover it up with when we moved on. The depth of the hole depended on how long we planned to stay. While we encamped, we covered the latrine with a stone; when we left, we filled it with dirt and strewed leaves over it. During our eighteen years together, Kozuka and I spent a great amount of time digging and covering up latrines.

Having no toilet paper, we had to use palm leaves instead. One time Shimada found some paper somewhere, but when he started to use it, Kozuka said, "You've only got enough for two or three times. Then you'll have to go back to leaves. Why bother?"

When we found leaflets that the enemy had dropped, we would save one of them and leave the rest where they were, so long as they all said the same thing. They made too much smoke to use for starting fires, and we were afraid to use them even for blowing our noses, because one piece of soiled paper might lead the enemy to us.

We often found cartoons or nude photos of women in the

mountains. They were not left by the search parties but deliberately distributed by the islanders. I guess they thought we would be tempted to take them, but we did not dare touch them for fear that we would reveal our location.

Fortunately, there was no malaria on Lubang. During my thirty years there, I was sick in bed with a fever only twice. Kozuka impaled his heel on thorns twice. Both times his leg swelled up, but otherwise he had no illnesses.

May is the hottest month in Lubang. In the daytime the thermometer goes up to about 100° Fahrenheit, and even if you sit still in the shade, the sweat pours off. If you have to walk fifty yards to get wood for the fire, you feel as though you were in a hot spring bath.

In June the squalls begin, coming up suddenly almost every day. Then in July, the real rainy season sets in. For two hours at a time it may rain so heavily that you cannot see more than ten yards away. This goes on for about twenty days, and sometimes the rain is accompanied by winds of nearly typhoon force.

In August there are more and more clear days, but the atmosphere is steaming hot. In September there is not much wind, but the rainfall is as heavy as in July. This goes on for about twenty days. Then there are blue skies for a day or two at a time over a period of two or three weeks, and finally in mid October the rainy season ends.

From then until the following April is the dry season. At first it rains a little once or twice a month; then there is no rain for several months. The coolest months are January and February, but even then the thermometer goes up to 85° or so in the daytime. The most comfortable time of the year is about like the hottest part of the summer in Tokyo. During this season only, we wore undershirts underneath our jackets.

In the dry season, we looked around the island carefully and decided where we would spend the next rainy season. There were several conditions that had to be met.

FOOD, WEATHER AND CLOTHING

Month	Vegetables & Fruits	Clothing	Temperature	Rainfall	Humidity	Winds
Jan.	papaya, banana, citron	3	4	0	0	9 W
Feb.	citron, *nanka*	3	4	0	0 ⎫ quite dry	10 W
March	rice from second crop, citron, *nanka*	2	5	0	0 ⎭	6 W
April	mango, citron, *nanka*	1	6	0	0	3 W
May	mango, citron, *nanka*	1	10	3 (showers)	9	0
June	mango, pineapple, citron, *nanka*, banana	1	8 86° F	1	8 ⎫ everything musty	0 ⎫ seasonal E
July	pineapple, banana	1 (2 if rain)	8 99° F	9	9 ⎬	2 (rain 8)
Aug.	banana	1 (2 if rain)	9	9 (sometimes 2)	9 ⎭	2 ⎭
Sept.	pineapple, banana	1 (2 if rain)	8	10	10	3 (rain 9) ⎫ seasonal W
Oct.	dry-field rice, *gaba*, pineapple, banana	2	7	4 (showers)	8	5 ⎬
Nov.	wet-field rice, *gaba*, citron, pineapple, banana	2	6	4	6	7 ⎭
Dec.	banana, pineapple, citron	3	5	1	2	8

Note: Ratings are on a scale of ten, except for clothing, in which case 1 indicates loincloth only, 2 indicates jacket and trousers, and 3 indicates jacket, trousers and underclothes.

The first, of course, was that the place had to be near a supply of food. There should be banana fields and coconut groves in the neighborhood, and the campsite should not be too far from a place where the cows grazed. At the same time, it had to be a spot to which the islanders did not come.

It also had to be a place where the smoke from our fire was not directly visible to nearby villages, and a little noise not audible. If possible, there should be a breeze. The most desirable location was on the cool eastern side of a mountain.

It was not easy to find a place that had all of the qualifications, and once we had found it, we had to go through a period of anxiety before we built our hut and settled in. The reason was that the rainy season was irregular. Some years it would rain all through May; other years we would be well into June before the first drop fell. If we built our camp before the rain started, there was a danger that the islanders would discover us. We had to wait until we were sure they would not come into the mountains.

When we thought the rainy season was about to start, we would go to the place we had picked to see whether we still thought it was all right. Then we would camp nearby until it began to rain, at which point we would set up our hut as rapidly as possible. We called the hut a *bahai*, the Tagalog word for "house."

The first step in building the *bahai* was to find a large tree to which the whole structure could be anchored. After we selected the tree, we stripped it of branches, which we used to build a frame. Rafters were placed slantwise against the ridgepole and covered with coconut leaves. The later were folded in two lengthwise and inserted between strips of split bamboo or palm branches. Everything was tied together with vines.

The *bahai* was built on slightly sloping ground, the upper part of the ground serving as the "bedroom." For beds, we first put down a few straight tree branches, then covered them with bamboo matting made by hand, and finally spread over the matting some duck sacks that we had requisitioned from the islanders.

The lower part of the *bahai* was the kitchen. Our "stove" consisted of several flat rocks placed together to form a platform for the fire and a pole above them from which our pot could be hung. Next to the hearth was a sheltered area where we could keep firewood and our rifles. Such walls as the *bahai* had were made of palm leaves, in the same fashion as the roof. Working with bolo knives, Kozuka and I could build the hut in seven or eight hours.

Before we started building huts like this in the early rainy season, we slept in tents, but often the wind blew the rain in until we were soaked and shivering all over. When that happened, we would warm ourselves up by singing army songs at the top of our voices. This was safe, because the noise of the wind and the rain drowned out the noise we were making. One of the songs we sang started with the words:

> Troops advancing in the snow,
> Tramping over the ice . . .

We were so cold at times like this that the song seemed appropriate, even on our snowless southern island.

The *bahai* was much more comfortable than the tents, but by the time the dry season approached, the roof had rotted so badly that a good deal of rain leaked through.

When the rainy season ended, we took the *bahai* apart and either burned the pieces or strewed them about in a hollow. Since it would not do merely to leave them there, we covered them with mud and spread branches and fallen trees over the spot. If we piled up a fair number of branches, they were enough camouflage to keep any islanders who might wander past from becoming suspicious.

We washed off the stones near the hut to remove any oil or

dirt and covered the ground where the hut had been with branches that we had saved for this purpose. It was particularly important that no one find the place until after we had time to move to a new location, so we pulled vines over the branches to make access as difficult as possible without making the camouflage obvious.

When Shimada, who was an energetic worker with plenty of strength, was still alive, we built our hut deep in the jungle. After his death, we usually settled for a place near the edge of the jungle. We also simplified the hut so that it would be easier to dismantle and hide. Actually, there were not so many satisfactory locations that fulfilled the most important condition, which was that we be near a banana field, and during the whole thirty years, we used the same few places three or four times each.

In the dry season, we slept in tents or in the open. When we stayed in the open, we picked a place with about a ten-degree slope, and Kozuka and I slept side by side. To keep from slipping downhill during the night, we put our baggage or a log below our feet. Our rifles were always within easy reach. We took off our shoes, but during the whole thirty years, I never once took off my trousers at night. I always kept a little pouch with five cartridges in it attached to my belt.

In the early stages, we covered ourselves at night with our tents or clothing. Later we sometimes used the dried hides of cows. At one point we had quilts of a sort that we had made by piecing together bits of rubber that had floated up on the south shore. If it suddenly started to rain while we were sleeping out, we simply got wet. There was nowhere else to go. When this happened, we were cold, and the next day the joints of my legs ached. If my midriff got cold at night, I usually developed a tendency toward diarrhea.

There was a big cave on Snake Mountain, and the islanders had built a number of cabins in the mountains near their fields,

Rainy season huts had to be anchored to a tree to keep them from blowing down. Five posts supported the roof of folded palm leaves. Ditches were dug at the lower end, for use as a fireplace, and along the sides, for drainage. Small piles of coconut lees (*lower right*) were used to keep ants at bay.

When it was not raining, I slept on mountain slopes where the inclination was ten to fifteen degrees. It was necessary to put my backpack or a log under my feet to keep from sliding down. I chose a place with bushes or trees for cover and slept fully clothed.

but we did not use these as shelters from sudden rains, because
there was too much danger of being discovered.

The reason why we slept on sloping ground was simply that
this way, if we were suddenly awakened, we could see what
was around us without raising up. Actually, during my entire
thirty years on Lubang, I never once slept soundly through the
night. When we slept on the ground outdoors, I shifted my
body often to keep my limbs from getting numb.

I kept a sort of calendar, which after thirty years was only
six days off the real calendar. My calendar was based largely on
memory and the amount of food left, but I checked it by looking
at the moon. For instance, if I picked ten coconuts on the first
of the month and we used one a day, the day we used the last
one would be the tenth. After making this calculation, I
would look at the moon and see whether it was the right size
for that day of the month.

When search parties were looking for us and we were moving
around every day, I tended to lose track of the date. When
that happened, I would start by looking at the moon and then
try, in consultation with Kozuka, to figure out how many days
had passed since some known date.

The moon was our friend in another respect as well, because
we usually moved from one encampment to another at night.
Kozuka often said, "The moon isn't on anyone's side, is it? I
wish the islanders were the same way!"

Our haircut routine was another help in keeping track of
the date. Kozuka once mentioned that back home the people
had always celebrated the twenty-eighth day of each month
as sacred to a local Buddhist deity. He said they had always
eaten a special noodle dish on that day. This reminded me that
when I was a boy, the barbers had always put out signs toward
the end of the year asking people to have their children's
hair cut by December 28 to avoid the year-end scramble. I
suggested to Kozuka that we commemorate his hometown's

monthly celebration by cutting our hair on the twenty-eighth of every month, and that is what we did. Somehow this seemed all the more appropriate to me because on the days when we did cut each other's hair, we were for a short while children again. Afterward, we often figured the date by counting the number of days since our last haircut. This was easy to remember.

We were particularly careful with the last haircut of the year, because it was a psychological boost to open the year with our heads looking spic and span.

On New Year's Day we made our own version of "red rice," that is, rice cooked with red lentil beans. This is served in Japan on festive occasions. We had no lentil beans, but there was a kind of string bean that grew on Lubang that we used as a substitute. On New Year's Day, we also made a special soup out of meat and papaya leaves, flavored with citron. This was intended as a substitute for the meat and vegetable soup called in Japanese *ozōni*, which is always served in the New Year season.

On the morning of the first day of the year, we bowed in the direction of the emperor's palace, which we considered to be north by northeast. We then formally wished each other a good year, renewed our pledge to do our best as soldiers, and repaired to our feast of "red rice" and *ozōni*.

We also celebrated our birthdays, and I remember one or two birthdays that I commemorated by giving myself a newly made cap.

Every morning I brushed my teeth with fiber from the palm trees. After I washed my face, I usually massaged the skin with kelp. When I wiped off my body, I often washed my underwear and my jacket at the same time. Since we had no soap, this amounted to rinsing the clothing in plain water, but sometimes I removed the grime from the neck and back of my jacket with the lye from ashes. I put the ashes in a pot and poured water over them. When the water cleared, I transferred it to a different pot and soaked the clothes in it. We had to be careful to hang our clothing in an inconspicuous place to dry.

There were several clear rivers, but during the whole thirty years I took a real bath only on those occasions when we cut up a cow and got blood and ooze all over ourselves. There is no such thing in the mountains as a valley with just a stream and nothing else. The valleys are also the roads. Except in the narrowest ravines deep in the mountains, we were afraid to undress to the skin, even at night. In the daytime, we bathed the upper parts of our bodies by pouring water over each other. In the evening we each washed off the lower parts of our bodies just before sunset. I would never have done anything so dangerous as to strip completely.

We took as good care of our guns and ammunition as we did of ourselves. We polished the guns with palm oil to keep them from rusting and cleaned them thoroughly everytime we had a chance.

In cool weather, the palm oil congealed. Then we just wiped off the guns and waited until later to oil them. When they got wet, they had to be completely disassembled and cleaned piece by piece. If there was no time for this, we oiled them liberally and waited for fair weather. Since exposure to water tended to make the butts rot, we occasionally had to remove the ammunition and hang the guns where the smoke from our fire would dry them out. The gun butts and slings gradually absorbed so much palm oil that the rats would gnaw at them, particularly the slings, and when we stopped at a place where there were lots of rats, we were forced to hang the guns out of reach on vines.

More troublesome than the rats were the ants. It would be no exaggeration to say that the mountainous section of Lubang

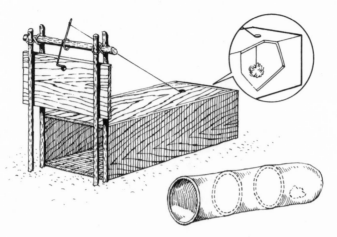

Two kinds of rattraps: the one at left was made of wood; the door would close when the bait was taken. The cloth bag at right was placed near my head when I slept. It would rustle when the bait was taken, then I would close it. The bait was coconut lees.

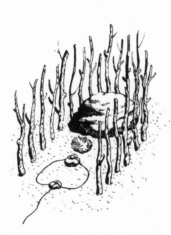 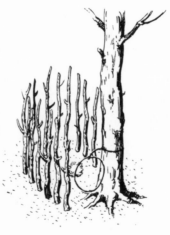

The snare at left was for jungle fowl, which tasted like pheasant. When the bird put its legs into the circle, the other end of the rope was pulled.

Right, a soft copper loop tied to a tree at the height of the animal's neck was effective for snaring wildcats.

was one enormous anthill. There were many varieties of ants. Some of them liked damp places; others thrived only where the ground was virtually parched. Certain types gathered together leaves to make their nests. To us, the biggest nuisance was a type of ant that carried about bits of dirt. These, the most numerous of all, were always crawling into our guns and leaving their dirt. If I just set my gun down for a while on top of my pack, almost immediately a stream of ants would start for the gun butt, and in the process some of them would enter the barrel and deposit dirt in the moving parts. Even a little dirt could cause the guns to jam. When the ants appeared, we would hang the guns from the branch of a tree. There was usually enough wind to keep them from being able to climb very high.

The ants also caused us bodily harm. There are at least five varieties that have stingers like those of bees. These attack the softer parts of the body, and if you are not immune, the sting swells up immediately. Once when I was stung inside the ear, my eardrum became so swollen that I could not hear with that ear for a week. The wound bled a number of times, and I had a fever.

Speaking of stings, there are also lots of bees on the island. Great swarms of them fly around the bushy area near the foot of the mountains like huge sheets. I have seen swarms thirty yards wide and a hundred yards long, flying along with "lookouts" fore, aft and on either side. If we came across one of these swarms, the only thing to do was make for the woods, or if there was not enough time, cover our heads with a tent or clothing and lie flat on the ground. If we made the slightest motion, they would attack. We had to breathe as lightly as possible until the swarm had passed over.

I was also bitten several times by centipedes. If one of these bites a person on the hand, his whole body swells up for a time; even after the swelling is gone, the bite takes a long time to heal. I was bitten on the right wrist in January, 1974, and the bite has not healed as I write these pages months later.

Under fallen leaves there were apt to be scorpions. When we slept outdoors, we always cleared off a place about three yards square, but even so I woke up in the morning several times to find a scorpion hiding under the rock I had used for my pillow.

Other unattractive residents of the jungle include snakes as big around as a man's thigh.

Every gun has its own quirks. At first the model 99 that I used for thirty years fired about a foot to the right and below the mark at a distance of three hundred yards. After a time I managed to fix the sights so that the aim was more accurate, but I was never able to reduce the error to less than three or four inches.

The stock of this gun was about an inch and a quarter shorter than normal, because at one point I had to remove the butt plate and cut off some wood that had rotted. After replacing the plate and putting in new screws, I was pleased to find that the gun was better suited to my size than before.

In the course of gunfights with enemy troops or islanders, we captured a carbine and a hunting rifle, but without ammunition they were useless to us, so we buried them deep in the jungle.

A slug from an infantry rifle travels about 670 yards in the first second after firing, but a carbine slug goes only about 500 yards in the first second. The islanders usually had carbines, and if we saw them fire on us from a considerable distance, we knew we had about one second in which to dodge. At night, you can even see a bullet approaching, because it shines with a bluish white light. I once dodged a flying bullet by turning my body sideways.

When Shimada was shot, Kozuka and I had to flee so rapidly that we left our bayonets behind. Later we found bayonets for Thompson machine guns in the house of an islander and filed down the bayonet holders on our guns so that these would fit. The file, incidentally, had been requisitioned.

Our ammunition pouches were fashioned from a pair of rubber sneakers. We first put the cartridges in cloth sacks tied at the top with strings. Each of us carried two sacks inside his pouch, one containing twenty cartridges, the other thirty. The top of the pouch came down over the sides and was fastened with a hook, like a camera case, to keep the contents dry. In addition to the ammunition in the pouch, I carried five cartridges with me in my pants pocket, and there were always five in the gun. Altogether, then, I was always armed with sixty cartridges, enough to enable me to make a getaway even if I stumbled across a fairly large search party.

I had six hundred rounds of machine gun ammunition, and in my spare time I fixed all the good ones so that they could be fired from my model 99. A lot of the bullets were faulty and had to be used for other purposes.

Since I could not use the repeater action on my gun with these modified cartridges, I fired them only when I was shooting a cow or firing a single shot to scare off islanders. There were about four hundred good cartridges in all, which I started using around the time Akatsu defected. They were about gone when I came out of the mountains twenty-five years later. I must have fired an average of only sixteen of them a year.

We were very careful about our spare ammunition. We kept it hidden in holes in the sides of cliffs, which we covered with rocks. We inspected the hiding places each year and at the same time put the ammunition in new containers. We marked the ammunition that was definitely good with a circle and that which was probably good with a triangle. We removed

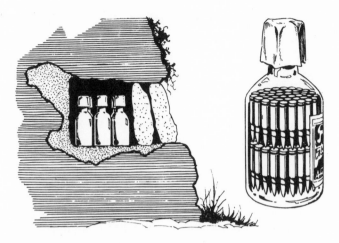

The storage of ammunition so that it would be in good condition when needed was very important. After the rifle and machine gun cartridges were stacked in bottles, they were covered with coconut oil. The bottles were hidden in caves, which were then covered with stones.

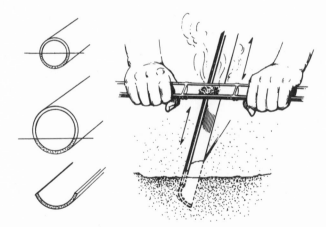

To make a fire at night or when it was dangerous to make smoke, I used split bamboo. One stick was planted firmly in the ground, and the other, holding coconut fiber and gunpowder, was rubbed vigorously up and down against it.

the powder from bullets that were too rusty to use and used it in building fires. It could be ignited with a lens we had requisitioned.

The containers for the ammunition were whiskey bottles and the like left here and there by the islanders. We used rubber from an old gas mask to stop up the bottles. For fear that rats might get in and eat the rubber, we also covered the mouths of the bottles with metal caps that we made from tin cans.

We tried to arrange the rocks covering the mouths of the storage holes to look as natural as possible, sometimes succeeding so well that we had trouble spotting them ourselves. In the course of a year, vines usually grew over them, and sometimes trees fell against them, almost concealing them. If we did not inspect at least once a year, there was a real danger that we might not be able to find them.

As can be seen from what I have said already, the worst years were the early ones, when we were not only afraid to make forays in the open but were at a disadvantage because of Akatsu's weakness. After Akatsu left, the remaining three of us adopted a more aggressive policy that called, among other things, for requisitioning more supplies from the islanders. They, for their part, were enjoying a rising standard of living, which meant that they not only had more goods worth stealing but also left more things about in the forest or in other reasonably accessible locations. Thus, our standard of living tended to rise in proportion to that of the islanders. Shimada's death deprived us of a faithful friend and a valuable worker, but it reduced the supply problem to some extent, if only because the meat from one cow will feed two longer than it will three. Life in the jungle was never easy, but so far as food, clothing and utensils were concerned, it was far easier in the later years than in the first five or ten.

DEVILS IN THE MOUNTAINS

In order to clear the way for the Japanese landing party that we continued to expect, we adopted guerrilla tactics aimed at enlarging the territory under our control and keeping out all enemy trespassers.

We conducted what we called "beacon-fire raids." We would go to various places in the early part of the dry season and burn piles of rice that the islanders had harvested from their fields in the foothills.

The season for harvesting this rice came in early October, around the time when we dismantled our rainy season dwelling and moved farther up into the mountains. From about halfway up we could see them cutting and bundling the rice. To protect it from the moisture, they spread thick straw matting on the ground and piled the unhulled rice on that. We would wait until twilight and then, approaching stealthily to a nearby point, fire a shot or two to scare the islanders away. This nearly always worked, and after they had fled, we set fire to the rice by sticking oil-soaked rags in the piles and lighting them with matches. We thought of the fires as beacons signaling to friendly troops who might be in the vicinity of Lubang that the "Onoda Squadron" was alive and carrying out its duties.

Matches, which were essential to this type of operation, were not always easy to obtain. They had to be requisitioned, of course, and it was important not to waste them. Whenever we acquired some, we first dried them thoroughly, then shut them up tightly in a bottle. In principle, we used them only for our beacon raids, relying at ordinary times on other methods, such as rubbing two sticks of bamboo together or igniting a little gunpowder from unusable ammunition with our lens.

The islanders would of course report our raid to the national police force stationed on the island, and the police would come running. We had only a short time in which to set our fire, seize whatever supplies the islanders had left behind, and beat it back into the jungle.

We thought that the local police would report our raids to the American forces, and that Japanese intelligence units would pick up the messages. The raids would, we reasoned, make it difficult for the Americans to neglect Lubang, while at the same time assuring our own people that we had the situation on the island under control. This would presumably make it possible for them to fight on, wherever they were fighting, without worrying about us. The raids would also help convey to the islanders the idea that it was dangerous for them to leave their villages and go into the foothills to work.

From the mountains, Kozuka sometimes called out toward a village, "Don't think you're safe because there are only two of us! One step too far, and you'll be in trouble!" No one could hear him, I suppose, but this was apparently good for his spirits.

Actually, burning the rice in the same places every year increased the danger that the islanders might anticipate our movements and set a trap for us. We therefore varied our tactics to some extent, putting off the raids for a month in some years or for five months in places where two crops were grown each year. We tried to keep them guessing as to where we might pop up. If we could nurture the fear that we might show up almost anywhere at almost any time, that in itself would accomplish half of our objective.

The eighteen years that Kozuka and I spent together were the ones in which I was most actively engaged in guerrilla tactics. This was due to a large extent to the rapport that existed between us. We nearly always saw things the same way, and frequently we needed only to look at each other to decide what we would do next.

Although I had not known Kozuka before I came to this island, the fortunes of war were such that we became closer than real brothers. I respected his spirit and his daring. He, for his part, deferred to me in matters of judgment. Many times we told each other that when our assignment had been carried out, we would return to Japan together. If by chance we never made contact with friendly forces, we would rot together on Lubang. We laughed as we talked over these two prospects.

Then at times when we had found some particularly fine bananas, or handily eluded a search party, or led the enemy a merry chase, we would suddenly say simultaneously, "If only Shimada were here!"

Besides carrying out our beacon raids, we decided to try to collect information directly from the islanders. To go anywhere where there were lots of people would be dangerous, but there were plenty of lonely spots on the island where we might take one of the farmers prisoner as he went to or from his fields.

We singled out a lonely farm hut near the salt flat in Looc. This was near the edge of the jungle, and it would be easy to escape if we ran into unforeseen trouble.

Coming out of the woods at the salt flat, we approached the hut, staying low and keeping a sharp eye on the surroundings, We looked in. Nobody was there, nor was there anything to requisition. Suddenly Kozuka, who had very good ears, whispered, "Somebody's coming!"

He pointed toward the ocean, and when I looked, I saw a man of about forty making his way through the tall grass toward us. We waited silently by the hut, rifles ready. When he was about three yards away, I leaped out in front of him with my rifle aimed straight at his chest. He let out a surprised yell, then raised his hands.

Kozuka told him in English to sit down, and he began talking quickly in Tagalog, which we could not understand. I motioned to him to shut up, and he did. We led him at gunpoint into the house. Somewhat to our relief, he made no effort to resist.

When I asked him why he had come here, he answered in a combination of English and Tagalog, with many gestures, "I left a dog near here to keep my cows from being stolen. I came to take the dog back. I'm not a Yankee spy. Don't kill me."

Not wanting to stay in the house too long, we took him into the mountains, where we questioned him thoroughly about conditions on the island. He told us everything he knew, down to the price of cigarettes and the average pay for a day's labor. Throughout the questioning, he continued to shake with fright. When we decided we had learned all we could, we told him to go home and go to bed. His face registered great relief.

In late 1965 we acquired a transistor radio.

It was in the farmlands on the shore opposite Ambil Island, where a number of islanders were putting up in a cabin for a few days to work on their fields. Among them was a man in neat white clothes, who kept going in and out of the cabin. As we watched from among the trees, we saw him work for about thirty minutes and then walk off toward the mountain opposite us. He was carrying a gun, and he was pretty big.

"Who do you suppose that is?" asked Kozuka.

"Probably somebody working for the army or the police," said I, and we decided to go after him. Before we moved, however, three more men showed up and made as though to join the man in white. The second they were all together, we fired a couple of shots to frighten them, sending them scurrying toward the jungle, two in one direction and two in another. Two more shots, and they disappeared, gathering speed as we lost sight of them. The remaining farmers also scattered.

We went into the deserted cabin and found not only a transistor radio but some good socks, shirts and trousers. The socks were of thin nylon and looked fairly expensive—too expensive at any rate to belong to any of the islanders, to whom nylon was still a novelty. These men had obviously come from somewhere else. We were all the more convinced of this because we did not think the islanders would bring a radio along when they came to work in the fields.

We requisitioned the radio and the other things and then went back into the jungle. The radio was a Toshiba eight-transistor set that seemed to be a very good one. The batteries in it were new, and there were four spare batteries. When we turned it on that night, the first thing we heard was a man saying in Japanese. "Today being December 27, this is my last broadcast of the year. Listen in again next year. In the meantime, Happy New Year to you all!"

It was Kinkazu Saionji, broadcasting from Peking.

The radio provided the first information about the outside world that we had had since the newspapers and magazines left by the 1959 search party, but we limited our listening time to conserve the batteries. For the first year, we listened only to the news as broadcast from Peking. After we acquired more batteries, we began listening to Japan Shortwave Radio, the South American broadcast from NHK, the Japanese-language broadcast from Australia and even the BBC from London.

The replacements for the batteries came from the flashlights that the islanders carried. The farmers sometimes worked late in the fields near the edge of the jungle, and if we fired a few shots to frighten them, they would usually run away leaving their flashlights behind. The flashlight batteries were too big to go in the radio, of course, but we made a plastic cylinder that would hold four of them and connected this to the radio.

When we had spare batteries, we melted a candle in the top of a can and dipped each end of the battery into the tallow to seal the terminals. They would stay good for about three years when we did this.

During the rainy season, we made an antenna out of about ten yards of copper wire strung between two trees at a height of about fifteen feet. The wire was stolen from the islanders, of course.

As in the case of the newspapers we had received, we did not believe anything we heard on the radio concerning military affairs or foreign relations. We considered that we were listening not to live broadcasts but to tapes made by the Americans, who had deleted or altered anything unfavorable to them. What pretended to be a broadcast from Japan or Australia was, to our way of thinking, a tape prepared by the enemy and rebroadcast with suitable changes. There were many people in the Philippines who understood Japanese, and the Americans were apparently trying to discourage those who might be sympathetic to Japan by broadcasting doctored Japanese-language programs that professed to come from Japan or other countries, but in reality presented the American viewpoint.

At one point, Kozuka remarked, "When you think of it, the Americans are really good at this, aren't they?"

"Yes," I replied. "They have to take out anything they don't want heard and then rebroadcast it in almost no time. They must have managed to gather together a bunch of very smart people. Just one slip, and the whole thing would sound fishy. I take off my hat to them. It must be very tricky work!"

Later, when I found out that the broadcasts had not been faked, it occurred to me that it had been "very tricky work" indeed for us to read into the news broadcasts the meanings we wanted them to have.

Aside from items having to do with military activities or foreign affairs, we thought that the programs we heard were genuine enough. We accepted, for instance, the idea that the Tokyo Olympic Games had been carried out successfully, and that Japan had a new "bullet-train" system in operation between Tokyo and Osaka. After all, people were always saying that there were no national boundaries in the world of sports, and it seemed plausible enough that the Olympic Games might be held even if there was a war going on. As for the new train line, I knew that even before the war there had been a plan to build a superexpress railway between Tokyo and Shimonoseki.

At the beginning of the rainy season in the year after we acquired the radio, Kozuka injured his foot. We had killed a cow, and as we were lugging the meat to our hut, he stepped on a thorn that went deep into his heel.

It must have been terribly painful. He said nothing, but his face was contorted and he turned deathly pale. Having no way of knowing what kind of poison the thorn contained, after I removed it, I pricked around the wound with a needle, forced out the blood, and then applied some American-made mentholatum, which we had picked up in an islander's house.

This was the second time Kozuka had hurt his foot. The first time had been around the time Akatsu had made his second attempt to leave, and I remembered how bad it had been then. I had a feeling that this second injury was going to be troublesome too.

I was right. The next day Kozuka's leg was swollen up to the thigh. After about a week, I breathed a sigh of relief when the swelling went down, but this was premature.

Thinking that the injury had healed, we decided to go fetch some batteries that we had hidden. Just as we reached the point near the Looc lookout tower where we had planned to spend the rainy season, Kozuka's leg crumbled under him, and he could not go on. I put up our hut myself and continued to apply cool packs to Kozuka's leg, sometimes massaging it lightly at the knee and calf to stimulate the blood flow.

Kozuka was in bed throughout the rainy season. During this period we listened often to the broadcasts of Japanese horse races on Japan Shortwave Radio, and Kozuka taught me the rudiments of horse racing. Even now I remember one running of the Japan Derby that was delayed from May until early July by a trainers' strike or something like that. Betting centered on three well-known horses, but Kozuka and I agreed that the horse ranked fourth looked like the winner.

"There are more than twenty horses in the derby," said Kozuka. "Anything can happen. I'll admit this horse isn't really as strong as the first three, but if his trainer didn't push him very hard on the day before the race, I think he'll run away from the pack and win before they catch him."

He did just that and won by six lengths. Kozuka and I were lost in self-admiration, particularly since the nag hardly won another race either before or after.

After Kozuka recovered enough to walk, we started betting with each other on the races. Whoever won on a given day made the decisions on the following day. A lot depended on luck, of course, but we reasoned that the man who picked the winner was also displaying superior intuition, and it made sense for him to take the leading role. As often as not, however, the broadcast was drowned out by static, and we did not hear the results.

We also listened to popular music programs. It seemed to me that most of the new singers had thin voices and had to stand very close to the microphone to be heard. I preferred the older singers, like Noriko Awaya, who had been singing the blues before the war. I heard a broadcast of her singing at Expo '70 in Osaka; it reminded me of listening to records of Chaliapin singing the "Volga Boat Song."

The singers I like today are the ones who sing of traditional subjects and put a lot of vigor in their performance. After I returned to Japan, I mentioned this to my brother Tadao, and he said, "You like the songs aimed at giving you more fight."

I suppose he was right, although I had never thought of it that way.

One of the programs that I always wanted to listen to was the big New Year's Eve show put on by NHK every year, in which all the leading singers participate. It was broadcast on shortwave, but we never listened to more than a part of it, because it runs for three hours, and we did not like to use the batteries that long.

To cheer Kozuka up while he was sick, we indulged ourselves somewhat in the radio, but that did not last long. The main trouble was that since we had to keep the volume low, we had to twist ourselves into unnatural positions to keep our ears close to the speaker. This could be very tiring. We decided that our bodies and the batteries were more important than the fun of listening to the horse races and music programs, and before long we gave them up almost entirely.

One difficulty with the Japanese language is that it has many words meaning "I" and "you," and they have to be chosen with care to fit the given situation. In the Japanese army, the common words for "you" were *kisama* and *omae*, both of which can easily sound insulting if not used with caution. We dodged this problem by using the Tagalog words *ako* for "I" and *ikao* for "you."

I tried very hard not to say anything that would make Kozuka angry, and he did the same toward me. There was no one around to intervene. Once we started fighting, it was bound to go on until both of us had it all out of our system. But our world had a population of two, both male, and every once in a while we did have bitter clashes, usually over something trivial.

"Just hold on a minute, Kozuka," I said. "I'm not going to take that lying down!"

During all my time in the army, I had never once sent Kozuka or any other of my men in front to protect myself. I could not let him get away with a nasty remark like that. I took off my pack and plopped down on the ground where I was.

Speaking quietly, I said, "I can get along by myself, and I can carry out my duties by myself. I'm grateful for all that I've learned from you and Shimada about living in the mountains, but I am an officer, and I am responsible for the war on this island. Up until now I've acted in accordance with my own judgment, and I'm prepared to take responsibility for what I've done."

Looking at me insolently, he said, "Second Lieutenant Onoda, sir! Keep it to yourself! I'm fed up with your sermons!"

"Sermons?" I countered. "I am merely stating facts. I'm simply pointing out to you where you're wrong."

"Why you lazy, good-for-nothing . . ."

He was so mad he could not go on. By this time, our Tagalog *ikao*s had given way to the most abusive army language, and I was almost as excited as he. Suddenly I realized that I was losing control of myself; shouldering my pack again, I walked on ahead. We both needed to go somewhere and cool off.

I had not taken ten steps when Kozuka threw a rock and hit me in the back. I whirled around and found him preparing to throw more rocks.

"Stop that, you idiot!" I shouted.

The command only made him worse, and he started raving.

"Who's an idiot? Not me. I'm no idiot! I know who's on my side and who isn't. You don't listen to me, so you're not on my side. You're an enemy! You're an enemy of Japan, and I'm going to kill you!"

I put my pack down again and looking straight into Kozuka's

eyes said, "We've been together a long time. Whenever I've given orders, it has been because I thought they were for the good of my country and my people. I consider you my comrade, and I've tried very hard all this time not to say anything that would harm you or hurt your pride. It hasn't always been easy, because I'm human too. And still, every once in a while you go into your song and dance about how my faulty leadership caused a lot of soldiers to surrender, how I undercut Akatsu, how I was responsible for Shimada's death.

"You don't know it, but whenever you go off on that tack, one of four situations exists. Either the weather is bad, or the enemy is stronger than we thought, or you're tired and discouraged because something hasn't gone according to plan, or chow is late and you're very hungry. It's only when one of those things happens that you get angry and start criticizing me. The situation today is number three—you're very tired, and a couple of things haven't gone the way you wanted them to.

"Why can't you be cooler and more objective? There are only the two of us, after all."

"Shut up!" he cried. "I told you I don't want any more sermons."

"All right then," I replied. "I've said what I had to say. If you still want to kill your only comrade, go to it. I'll do you the favor of dying for you. But after I'm dead, it's up to you to go on living. It's up to you to fight twice as hard to cover my share."

Rough waves were breaking in the ocean nearby, but I could not hear anything. I do not think Kozuka could either. All sound around us was shut out; we faced each other in silence.

Thirty or forty seconds passed, and Kozuka said quietly, "Lieutenant, you lead the way."

Those words made us closer comrades than we had been before. I nodded silently and started off on the rocky path.

The islanders called us the "mountain bandits," the "kings of the mountain," or the "mountain devils." No doubt they had good reason to hate us.

One year just before the rainy season we stopped for a few days about halfway up Snake Mountain. At one point we decided to "step out" to the nearby village and look for supplies. We hid our packs and around sundown started down the mountain. Coming out at a spot somewhere between Vigo and Malik, we peered from the safety of a small hillock out over the nearby fields. We saw a young girl with a bandanna around her head and a boy in an undershirt and shorts. They appeared to be watering the vegetables growing in the field. It was already fairly dark, and if they were still working in the field, they must live nearby.

Keeping our bodies low and moving closer, we soon saw the roof of a nipa house nestled among the banana trees. We had never seen the house before and wondered when they had built it.

When we came out of the bushes, we saw the girl walking toward the house beyond the banana field. The boy had disappeared. The girl went into the house and soon came out again with a man who appeared to be her father. They started preparing their dinner on an outdoor hearth near the door. We slipped up behind them and forced them at gunpoint back into the house. Inside was a darkish, dingy room where an elderly woman, presumably the mother, stood motionless with fright as she watched us. We began searching the hut, but there were only a few articles of men's clothing among a lot of women's things.

I motioned for the man to give me his flashlight; trembling with terror he handed it over. The battery was so near dead that it was useless. The only food to speak of was some unpolished rice, and we found neither sugar nor cigarettes. Near the back of the room there was a pair of new basket-weave sandals, which I took.

"There's nothing else here," I said, "so we may as well go back."

But at that point the man started talking in Tagalog, and I gathered that he wanted to go outdoors and take his pot off the fire. I nodded permission, and the girl and her father tumbled out of the house as though they were falling from a ladder. After the man had removed the pot, he said something that seemed to mean that the rice was just right, and then he offered it to us.

"Should we eat it?" asked Kozuka.

"Why not?" I replied.

The girl had gone back into the house. We thought she was helping her mother prepare something to go with the rice, but when we looked inside, we found that the mother was gone. We immediately saw where the woman had removed a floor board and crawled out on the other side of the house, doubtless to run for the police. That did not seem to matter much, because it would be some time before they arrived, and we could eat in the meanwhile.

Just as we were finishing, the mother came back. We knew it was time for us to leave, but somehow we felt we ought to pay the woman back for her treachery. Scowling, we pointed our rifles at the girl and the father, and I said, "You're coming to the mountains with us."

Upon hearing that, the girl sank to the floor and got a tight hold on the doorpost. The father started pointing to the rice pot to remind us that he had fed us.

Kozuka and I shook our heads in rejection of his plea, and I took out a match as if to set fire to the house. The daughter started talking in Tagalog. I could not understand her, but I suppose she was praying, because at the end she said "Amen."

The natives on the island were almost all Catholic, and there was a picture of Christ on the wall.

I said, "I guess we've scared them enough. After all, they did give us dinner. Let's beat it!"

But just then I heard the report of a gun, and a bullet tore through the roof. The mother and daughter flattened themselves out on the floor, and the man ran out of the house. For a moment we considered staying and putting up a fight, but it seemed like a spendthrift way to use ammunition. We ran out the door and made straight for the jungle, keeping low to avoid the fire that we could hear behind us. After running about a hundred yards, we dived into a thicket of trees, where we stopped to catch our breath. The police did not pursue, and from there on we climbed the mountain at our customary pace, grumbling to ourselves about having been reported on the sly. Kozuka was so angry that he threw the basket-weave sandals into a clump of bushes and left them. As we proceeded toward Snake Mountain, we could still hear sporadic fire. Once when we looked back, we saw flashlight beams crossing each other back and forth.

Several months after that, we discovered that the islanders were coming in large numbers to the Vigo River valley, and we went to a hut near the quarry at Tilik to scare them away. On the way back, we were surprised by the police, who had received an early report of our foray, and who now had us in a crossfire from a distance of only about thirty yards. We escaped by diving into some *gaba* hedges, but one bullet ricocheted into my ankle and wounded me slightly.

When we reached our base, I opened the brand-new waterproof tent that I had found at the hut and discovered that the lettering on it said "Mitsubishi Trading Company." This was gratifying, because it confirmed our belief that war and commerce were being carried on independently of each other. At the same time, the police at Tilik had moved against us with such speed that we decided to be more careful in the future.

On the last day of every year, we went to a river and washed all of our clothes. Like most Japanese, I set great store by the New Year's celebration, and in that season at least I liked to have on fresh, clean clothing. The year-end washing was one of the major events on my private calendar.

On the last day of 1971, we did our washing in the middle reaches of the Agcawayan River, where the water was clear and rapid. As it turned out, this was my last New Year's Eve with Kozuka. The location was not far from Wakayama Point, where I encountered Norio Suzuki in February, 1974.

We started washing before the sun was well up. We did our caps, our jackets, trousers, loincloths, stomach wrappers and leggings—everything that we were not wearing at the time. As we were finishing up, Kozuka exclaimed in alarm, "My pants are gone! They must have been carried off by the current."

This could be very bad. The river flows down into a village called Brol, but even if the pants did not get that far, they were very likely to be spotted by islanders fishing between the village and where we were. Our whereabouts could easily be guessed at, but aside from that, we were vain enough not to want to give the islanders a close look at the patched-up clothing we were wearing. We started running down the river, splashing water all over ourselves. We ran a hundred yards, two hundred yards, five hundred yards, but no sign of the pants. We made our way back upstream, looking slowly and carefully all the way, but the trousers were not to be found.

Kozuka began to grumble, "If you didn't insist on doing this big washing to mark the end of the year, this wouldn't have happened. We're soldiers. What does the New Year's celebration mean to us? We shouldn't have done all this washing!"

I pointed out to him that it was he who had lost the pants,

not I, and that this was no time to be grouching. We had to decide quickly whether to try to find the pants before some islander found them or move on immediately to a new location.

"You're starting to preach again," complained Kozuka, and I saw that he was on the verge of blowing up.

"All right, all right," I told him. "We can talk about it some other time. Right now I want to try to find the pants if we possibly can. You follow along on the riverbank with your gun, while I go down the river searching the bottom and everywhere else. They're bound to be somewhere."

He consented, and I jumped into the river wearing the nylon shirt I had planned to wear on New Year's Day. We started down the river again, and this time I dived in all the deep places, while Kozuka made his way along the bank in the shade of the trees, keeping watch on both sides of the stream.

We spent about two hours on the pants search, to no avail. After we had climbed back up to the place where we had done our washing, I took off my shirt and threw it into the water with the intention of rinsing it out. To my utter astonishment, the shirt started floating slowly upstream. For a moment I thought I was losing my mind. Then I suddenly realized that the shirt was in an eddy. I watched it move upstream for about thirty yards, gathering speed as it went, until it reached a sharp curve in the river, where it seemed almost to be sucked around the bend. Jumping into the river once again, I followed the eddy up to where it began, and there, caught in the branches of a tree that had fallen across the stream, were Kozuka's pants, looking rather like a dying animal crouched in the water. Needless to say, I also recovered my shirt.

Turning around, I held up the pants so that Kozuka could see them. He waved his gun in the air, a broad grin on his face.

After we cut some coconuts, the milk of which we planned to drink the next morning in lieu of the customary New Year's sake, we gathered up our belongings and went back to our encampment. I had been in the water so long that I was afraid I would catch cold, so I asked Kozuka to lend me his jacket, which was dry. He quickly consented, and when I put the jacket on, it warmed me to the bottom of my heart.

That New Year's Eve and the one on which I arrived on Lubang in 1944 were the most memorable during the whole thirty years.

ALONE

I shall never forget October 19, 1972 (October 13 by my calendar), for that is the day Kozuka was shot down.

About ten days before that, we dismantled our rainy season *bahai* and started up from the Looc area by way of Brol toward the ridge of which Twin Mountains was a part. We usually carried out our beacon raids between about October 5 and Octover 20, but this year we were late because the rainy season was slow in ending. As we walked, we speculated on how the delay would affect our plans.

We hid for one day at a spot from which we could see the whole central ridge, and in the evening we started cautiously uphill. It may be that some of the islanders sighted us then, because the next day the police showed up much more quickly than usual.

On that day, we peered out from our hiding place and saw the farmers harvesting their dry-field rice on the slopes below us. We intended that first day only to size up the lay of the land preparatory to making our bonfires on the following day. Somehow, however, it looked as though the islanders were planning to complete their work today, and if they did, the rice would not be there the next evening. For us, that would mean waiting another month or so until the rice in the wet fields was harvested.

"What should we do? Shall we burn at least one place today?"

"Yes. We've come this far, so let's go ahead and do it."

From the height where we were, we could see the town of Tilik and the sea stretching out beyond. Since there was a village not far away, we would have to start our beacon fires in a hurry. Still, no matter how quickly the islanders reported our presence, it would take the police at least ten minutes to arrive on the scene. Assuming that we could ignite one pile of rice in about three minutes, we should be able to light three piles and still have time to get away.

Partly to test some of our more suspicious bullets, when we approached the fields, we tried to fire several shots in the air. As we had thought, the first five or six rounds did not fire, but eventually one did. At the sound, two islanders in the fields took off in the opposite direction, as did a third who was on the neighboring ridge to our right. That left the place unguarded, and when we made sure that the frightened farmers had not turned back toward us, we lit our first fire. As Kozuka set fire to another small pile of rice, I gathered up what the islanders had left behind. There were two bolo knives, some cigarettes, some matches and even some coffee—not a bad haul at all. We started back on the other side of the ridge, where we could not be seen from the nearby village. On a little rise, we saw a large *doha* tree, and Kozuka said, "There's a pile of rice under that tree."

I looked, and there was indeed a pile of rice sacks. Nearby someone had gathered together three flat rocks to serve as a fireplace, and a pot was hanging down from a branch of the tree over this. There did not seem to be anyone around.

Kozuka murmured, "Don't you suppose the police will be arriving soon?"

I answered, "Yes, it's about that time."

"Those idiots are always getting in the way! Let's just sneak in one more fire."

"All right, let's give it a try."

We went up to about five yards from the tree and put down our packs, laying our rifles on top of them. Since the rice was in sacks, we needed some straw matting or something like that to put over them, or else the fire might not start. We looked around, and on the slope toward the village, we spotted a piece of straw matting that would just fill the bill. Kozuka went to get it, and I went to see what was in the pot. Just as I took the pot from the branch, I heard gunshots on both sides of me, and they were very close. We were too late!

I dived headfirst to the place where we had left our rifles and seizing mine, rose on my knee to take aim. The enemy was firing like mad. I knew from the sound that they were using carbines and small automatics. There were hills around where the shrubs grew thickly, and if we moved fast, we would be all right.

Kozuka also hit the dirt near me and reached for his gun. He grasped it, but then drew his hand back. I thought maybe the front sight was caught in the baggage, and when Kozuka reached out again, I shifted my own rifle to my left hand and pulled his gun forward to make it easier for him to reach. But again Kozuka drew back his hand, and his rifle stayed in mine.

"It's my shoulder!" he cried. Startled, I looked at him without altering my stance. There was blood coming from his right shoulder.

"If it's only the shoulder, don't worry! Get back down into the valley."

The enemy was still firing. Holding Kozuka's gun, I turned in the direction the bullets were coming from. From the shadow of some bushes about 120 yards away, two figures suddenly emerged, letting out a battle cry. I decided they must be islanders who had brought the police here, and from the sound of the next shot, I concluded that the police must be to the left and a little in front of the islanders. I fired three or four rapid shots in that direction, and the enemy's fire broke off. That gave me my chance. Grabbing the two guns I turned to flee.

Kozuka was still standing in the same place! I thought he would have backed down five or ten yards while I was returning fire, but he was still there, arms folded and apparently pressing against his heart.

I started to scream to him to get down, but before I could open my mouth, he sobbed, "It's my chest."

Chest? Did they get him twice?

Kozuka groaned, "It's no use!"

As I looked, his eyes went white. A second later, blood and foam spewed out of his mouth, and he fell over forward.

To gain time, I tried to fire the five bullets in my rifle, but the fourth one just clicked without firing. Without thinking, I stopped shooting.

I called to Kozuka, but there was no answer. He did not budge. I let go of my rifle and shook him by the ankle, but there was no response. Was it all over? Was he really dead? I tried one more time to call him, but I could not speak.

Hard as it was to face, if his eyes turned white and blood spewed from his mouth, he was dead. There was nothing more I could do. I took the two rifles and ran about fifteen yards down the slope to a thicket. From there I looked back at Kozuka, but he was still lying there, just as he had been.

I gave up and hurried down into the valley. The gunfire continued behind me. I ran through the forest, shouting, "I'll get them for this! I'll kill them all! Kill them, kill them, kill them!"

Now there was no one left but me. Shimada had been killed. Kozuka had been killed. My turn was next. But I vowed to myself that they would not kill me without a fight.

There was a coconut grove in the mountains about three-quarters of a mile from where Kozuka had been shot. I went there and on a nearby slope sorted out our equipment. Until then Kozuka and I had each been carrying about forty-five pounds, but now that I was alone, there were items that I did not need anymore. I put the things I needed together and buried the rest in the ground.

About the time I finished this, I heard voices nearby. Grabbing the two rifles, I moved stealthily in the direction of the sound. There was a work hut in the coconut grove, and five or six islanders were milling around. The sight of them filled me with anger; I thought of killing them all on the spot. I decided against firing, however, mostly because it was not easy to move around while holding two rifles.

Not long afterward, I saw fifteen or sixteen islanders walking along on the ridge where Kozuka had been killed. They were babbling excitedly, and once again I was filled with rage, but I reflected that there were probably policemen around, and anyway the islanders were a good seven hundred yards away from me.

"Take it easy," I told myself. "This is not the right time." But I swore that one day I would kill them all.

The next day I coated Kozuka's rifle heavily with coconut oil and greased the barrel with some pomade that I had hidden away. To keep the rats from eating the butt, I covered it with some sheet metal and hid the rifle away in a crevice between some rocks. I also put away the made-over machine gun bullets I had been using and replaced them with real 99 bullets. As I was doing all this, I could not keep Kozuka's blood-spewing face out of my mind.

I remembered that there had been five enemy volleys between the first shot and the time when I ran down into the valley. A carbine fires fifteen rounds at a time, and if the enemy had three carbines, as I suspected, there would have been forty-five rounds in each volley, or a total of 225 rounds, I decided that Kozuka must have been hit on the first volley.

It could not have been more than two seconds between the time he was hit and the time he dived for his gun. Another five or six seconds elapsed between the time when he said, "It's my shoulder," and the time when he fell over. He must have died only eight seconds or so after he was hit. What must have gone through his mind during those last eight seconds?

As I put away Kozuka's rifle—this rifle that he had had by his side continually for twenty-eight years—it was difficult to suppress the emotions that rose within me.

On the same day I moved to Kumano Point and settled down for a few days about two hundred yards northwest of the spot where I later built my mountain hut. As I was looking around, a helicopter appeared in the sky and started flying back and forth over the island. I decided that a new search party had come, and that it must be a fairly big one.

Hiding among the trees, I took stock of my position.

When I was just staying in one place, there was no doubt but that being alone was a disadvantage. On the other hand, if I was on the move, being alone had its good points. I was free to go where I chose, and I could travel lighter. Furthermore, it was easier to find food for one, and the danger of being discovered was correspondingly reduced. It was good to have an extra rifle, but I had already decided that the second one was more of a hindrance than a help when I needed to act rapidly. At the same time, the increased supply of ammunition made it easier to fight on a long-term basis. Feelings and emotions aside, I came to the conclusion that from the objective viewpoint, I was on balance about as well off as I had been. There was not so much difference between two soldiers and one soldier, so far as material things were concerned.

At any rate, this is what I wanted to think. I resolved once again that if I encountered the enemy, I would shoot to kill. If I did this, the islanders would be frightened and stay out of my territory. That in itself would make life easier.

But I never really carried out this plan, because I was interrupted by a new search party, which arrived only three days
after Kozuka's death.

"Onoda-san, wherever you are, come out! We guarantee
your safety."

So came the pleas from the search party's loudspeakers,
over and over again. It kept coming closer, and I became
convinced that I had to dodge the searchers somehow. I
moved eastward across the Vigo River, but to judge from the
movements of the helicopter, the search was being centered
on the mountains between Tilik and the radar base, in which
case I would not be able to escape unless I went to the area
between Agcawayan and Looc.

The islanders had finished harvesting their dry-field rice and
were beginning to harvest the rice in the wet paddies. Crawling
along the barriers between the paddies, I managed to gather
enough unhulled rice to last for a time, taking only a little
from each sheaf so as to avoid discovery. Then I started toward
the east, planning to make the trip in easy stages, stopping for
four or five days at a time. The more I thought about this,
however, the more I became convinced that I would have
trouble eluding the search party's dragnet. Eventually I
decided on a more aggressive line of action.

On the evening of November 19, just a month after Kozuka
was killed, I walked out into the open on the automobile road
at Ambulong, directly below the radar base. Presently I met an
islander going home from work. I uttered a threatening noise
and pointed my rifle at him. Thunderstruck, the man fled, but
he kept looking back at me and waving his arms as though
he were pleading for mercy. This in itself was unusual, because
when the islanders saw me, they always fled without looking
back. I decided that the man must have been told to make
sure it was me he had seen.

That suited me all right. I chased him, still training my rifle on him. Again he looked back, only to find that I had gained on him and was still prepared to shoot. He ran on for a while at full speed and then darted into one of the residences attached to the radar base.

I figured that when the man informed the search party he had seen me, they would come in large numbers to the road, and I would sneak off in the mountains toward Looc.

Just as I planned it, in about twenty minutes the search party showed up. Over their loudspeaker they said, "We had a report that you had shown up here, and we think you are somewhere where you can hear this speaker. . . . Onoda-san, if you don't believe we are Japanese, load up your infantry rifle before you come out."

I had to laugh. Load up my rifle indeed! The rifle that had been kept loaded for nearly thirty years. I was here, all right, and I could hear their loudspeaker. But I was not about to fall for something like that!

I crossed a branch of the Vigo River and made off in the direction of Looc. Then, from somewhere around Kumano Point, there came a woman's voice. I could not make out exactly what it was saying, but I caught the words, "Hiroo, you gave me two, didn't you?"

I recognized the voice as belonging to my older sister Chie, and I thought she must be talking about a pair of pearls that I had given her as a wedding present. While I was wondering about this, a man's voice came from another direction: " . . . a warrior, fight like a warrior! Soldier, fight like a soldier!"

It was my brother Tadao's voice, and I had heard these words at the Kurume Officers' Training School. So Tadao had come all the way from Brazil!

Still, that did not surprise me very much. I had learned from a leaflet that he had moved to Brazil. I remembered looking at a picture of him and his children in the leaflet and thinking that it was like him to go somewhere like that. I had always rather expected him to go to New Guinea or some other new country and get into development work. Brazil fitted in.

"It was good of him to travel such a long distance for my sake," I thought. "I think I'll just sit here and listen to him for a while."

I sat down where I was and tried to hear what he was saying. Because of the terrain and the wind. I could not make out everything the loudspeaker said, but I caught enough to know that Tadao was talking with his customary eloquence. He had once won the All-Japan Middle School Debating Contest, and he seemed to be making good use of his experience in that field.

I decided to postpone going to Looc and stay a while longer on the east slope overlooking the Vigo River. I had plenty of food, and there now seemed to be no great hurry to go to Looc. I might as well stay here and observe the search party a little longer.

At the time of the 1959 search party, I thought someone had been imitating my brother Toshio's voice, but this time the voices, both Chie's and Tadao's, were definitely theirs. This seemed to mean that the new search party had actually come from Japan and not from the American intelligence corps. I wanted to make sure of this point.

One evening about two weeks later, on the forty-fifth day after Kozuka's death, I went over to the place where he had been shot, with the intention of saying a prayer to comfort his spirit. Presumably the search party had wearied of looking here. Their activities in the area had all but ceased; I could hear no pleas from the loudspeaker.

As I came out of the bushes and approached the small hill from the rear, I found a book with the rising sun on the cover. On the flyleaf, in my brother's hand, there was a message saying, "You probably have things to say to me before we talk together. Tear out the flyleaf and write them down on it. If you leave it here, I'll receive it."

The writing was without doubt Tadao's, and I was now completely convinced that he was on Lubang.

Here, near Kozuka's grave, I was afraid that there might be enemy guards around. I kept hearing a noise that I was not accustomed to. Releasing the safety lock on my rifle, I walked cautiously on, my pack still on my back.

Last year, walking along a road that the islanders had built to make it easier to transport their rice, I had sung to myself a song about wartime comrades:

> My friend lies under a stone in the field,
> Lightened by the soft rays of the evening sun. . . .

After making sure no one was around, I looked up and in the darkness made out a Japanese flag flapping in the breeze. This was the odd noise I had heard. I sighed with relief.

As I drew near the *doha* tree, I saw that a large tombstone had been erected at the spot where Kozuka had fallen. Peering so closely that my face almost touched the stone, I made out large engraved characters saying: "Death Place of Army Private First Class Kinshichi Kozuka." Before the tombstone someone had placed a wreath of flowers and some incense. I knew from the way the marker had been set up that it had been placed there by Japanese.

I clasped my hands in prayer as I silently spoke to Kozuka: "I made things difficult for you, didn't I? You must have suffered a lot. I'm sorry I had fights and arguments with you. Go back to Japan ahead of me, and don't worry about me. I will avenge your death whatever happens. Being alone has not made me weak. Be at peace."

In my ears rang his last words, "It's no use!" I was all tight in the chest.

The moon came up, and in its pale light I could make out the outlines of Ambil Island in the distance. As I came back from the hill, I thought again of the song about comrades:

> Faithful to the Five Teachings,
> Lying a corpse on the battlefield.
> From old the warrior's conviction:
> Though not one single hair remains,
> No one can regret dying for honor.

I sang under the moonlight until my mind was at rest again. As I sang, I thought repeatedly of the pledge I had made before Kozuka's tombstone.

To avoid danger, I decided again that I must leave the vicinity of Kozuka's grave as soon as possible. I fixed on Agcawayan plain as my destination.

Next day around noon, I reached the plain and saw a Japanese flag flying in the middle of it. Apparently this was the search party's current headquarters.

I decided that on the following morning I would leave my hiding place before eating and go up in the valley for fresh water, taking a look around as I did so. In the course of carrying out this operation, I found a large number of discarded dry-cell batteries, as well as books, newspapers and leaflets. I picked these up and started back for my hideout but discovered to my surprise that I could not find it. There were a lot of little ridges around there; they all looked pretty much alike. I began to worry. I had my gun with me, but I had left behind all my spare ammunition. If it was found, the enemy would know where I was.

I do not remember ever being so frantic. It took me until the next day at noon to locate the hiding place. Sweating as much from anxiety as from heat, I must have searched every hill in the area except the right one, and at times I was no more than fifty yards away from it.

This would not have happened if Kozuka had been around. If there had been two of us, one of us would have stayed in the hiding place and would have seen the other searching for it.

The newspapers devoted a lot of space to Kozuka's death, and I went over all the articles very thoroughly. They said, among other things, that I myself seemed to have received a leg injury in the skirmish. That was untrue, and there were a number of other discrepancies in the stories.

What struck me as most peculiar was that none of the newspapers said a single word about Kozuka's "thousand-stitch waistband," which he had worn every day during his years on Lubang. A "thousand-stitch waistband" was a piece of cotton cloth in which each of a departing soldier's family and friends sewed one stitch, often attaching a coin or writing a short inscription. Many Japanese soldiers wore bands like this around their waists for good luck, and Kozuka was never without his. The newspapers not only failed to mention the waistband, but made the mistake of reporting that Kozuka had had a five-sen piece and a ten-sen piece *in his pocket*, when in fact they had been attached to the waistband. It looked to me as though the error must have been made on purpose. In any event, I came to the conclusion that these newspapers, like the others, had been doctored.

Kozuka's waistband had been a length of pink cloth on which there was a picture of a tiger. The coins, which his family had given him as good-luck pieces, were sewn on with red thread. Kozuka once told me, "I had to leave suddenly, and I had to use this cheap store-bought cloth. There wasn't time to make a proper 'thousand-stitch waistband.' It's terrible material. I'm surprised it is still holding together. There ought to be a law against merchants selling this flimsy pink rayon to soldiers going to the front."

Every year near the end of the rainy season, we repaired our clothes, and I remembered that this year I had seen Kozuka make a strong black waistband and wrap the pink one in it.

Why the newspapers would suppress the information about the waistband was a mystery to me. After pondering over this for some time, I arrived at a tentative conclusion.

Unlike the search party of 1959, the new expedition was actually sent by the Japanese goverment. The search, however, was only a pretext, the real purpose being to send a team of Japanese reconnaissance experts to conduct a detailed survey of Lubang. According to the news on the radio, Japan had become a large economic power, and it might well be that one aim of the search party was to spread a lot of money around Lubang and win the islanders over to the Japanese side. The appeals to me to come out, then, were intended to throw American intelligence off the track. Under cover of the ostensible search for me, Japanese agents would photograph every strategic point on the island and prepare detailed reports on the terrain and conditions among the people.

Looked at from this viewpoint, the pleas urging me to come out really meant that I should *not* come out, because if I came out, the game would have to end.

I knew from the radio that the Americans had failed badly in Vietnam, and it occurred to me that Japan might have seen that debacle as an opportunity to woo the Philippines over to the Japanese side. The Philippine government, for its part, might well be in the mood to switch its support from America to Japan. It stood to reason that the Japanese strategic command might have selected Lubang, where I was still holding out, as the place to establish a foothold in the Philippines. Hence the phony search party.

If I were to accept the search at face value and give myself up, the "search party" would have to go back to Japan without having accomplished its real objective. I had felt tempted by my brother's appeal, but it would not do for me to spoil the larger plan by giving in.

Mentally, I addressed words of encouragement to the "search party": "I will keep hidden where you won't find me, so survey the island as closely as you can. Working in a large group, you can find out much more about the mountains and the towns and the airfield than I could ever learn alone. If you win the support of the islanders and render the island harmless, my objectives will have been accomplished all the more quickly."

One thing that troubled me was that the members of the search party always seemed to be accompanied by armed Philippine soldiers. Why would intelligence agents sent from Japan always have Philippine guards with them? Was this not as much as telling me that they were enemies?

I was ninety-nine percent convinced that the "search party" had been sent from Japan. The remaining one percent remained hesitant because of those armed Philippine troops.

The helicopters kept flying noisily over the island and dropping countless leaflets in the jungle. The search party pitched tents in various locations and communicated with each other by telephone. As I moved about from hiding place to hiding place, I wondered why they did not leave me some binoculars and a telephone. If I had a telephone, I could talk to the intelligence agents in secret and relay to them all the information I had gathered over the years. The only explanation I could accept for their not leaving me a telephone somewhere was that they wanted at all costs to keep me from coming out of the jungle.

Looking at it from another angle, if they really wanted me to come out, they should have left not only a telephone but a machine gun and ammunition. If they had done so, I could have loaded the machine gun and walked right out in front of them. If they were really Japanese agents working for the same cause as I, they had no reason to fear that I would shoot. I was convinced that the war was still going on, and if the searchers wanted to prove they were friends, they had only to furnish me a weapon and ammunition. There could be no better proof.

I kept as far away from the search party as I could. Having stopped for a time near the shore south of Looc Bay, I proceeded to a hill from which I could look down on White Lady's Field, and there I celebrated the beginning of 1973. It was the first time I had seen in the New Year alone since my arrival on the island. Even with no one else around, I prepared my version of the Japanese "red rice."

On January 3 I left the hill, planning to move up toward Tilik by way of the Agcawayan plain and Wakayama Point. A day or two later, while I was still en route, I suddenly heard the sound of recorded music coming from the ridge in front of me. I moved to a point about five hundred yards away and spent one night. The following day near Wakayama Point I heard the record again. This time I decided to investigate.

That evening I approached the rice field where the loudspeaker was located. Someone had pitched a tent there, and I could tell by shadows from the light inside that people were moving around. I hid in a grove only about 150 yards from the tent and tried to hear what was being said.

It was my brother's voice again. Calling me by my childhood nickname, he said, "Hironko, this is Tadao. Many of the search party have left, and the soldiers who are here are only to protect us. They are not trying to kill you. If a Philippine soldier pointed his gun at you, I would jump in front of it and prevent him from shooting.

"I know you have had the experience of seeing Kozuka killed before your eyes, and I don't suppose you would believe anything I say. But if you don't get in touch with us, there is nothing we can do. Be brave! Act like an officer!"

I listened to my brother broadcasting two nights in a row, but I interpreted this also to mean the opposite of what he was saying about coming out of the mountains. My brother was an army officer, and he certainly knew what my orders were.

Three months passed after Kozuka's death. The survey appeared to have been nearly completed, because I rarely caught sight of the "search party" anymore.

I kept expecting a secret agent to come and establish contact with me. Maybe the attack on the Philippines had already begun. Whether it had or not, there should be some significant change in the near future.

But nothing happened. As I thought about this, it occurred to me that perhaps Lubang alone had declared itself independent and appealed for protection to the East Asia Co-Prosperity League. After all, even the little island of Nauru was now independent. If America could no longer be depended on, it stood to reason that the Philippines might ally themselves with the league, but even if that had not happened, it was possible that Lubang had become independent and come under the league's protection. But if that were the case, there would be no reason why a Japanese base could not be built here.

All in all, I decided I had better stay in hiding and wait a while longer.

In the latter part of February, the loudspeaker appeals started again. This was the third search party, and I knew from leaflets that it included fellow students from primary and middle school, as well as soldiers who had been at Futamata with me.

For a while I stayed in a place northwest of Kumano Point where I could hear the broadcasts, but afterward I moved to Wakayama Point and then to Kainan Point on the south shore.

From there I saw on the beach a yellow tent flying a Japanese flag and a slightly smaller Red Cross flag. Some people offshore in a native craft were calling out over the loudspeaker that they were from Kainan Primary School.

I began to wonder whether my brothers or these friends knew that they were being used by the Japanese strategic command. If they were consciously putting on this show, they must feel rather shabby about it. On the other hand, if they were sincerely making this appeal without knowing the real purpose, I felt sorry for them.

Two months later the island quieted down again. Six months had passed since Kozuka's death, and I thought that by now the survey must certainly be finished. Toward the end of April, by way of checking on whether the search party had really left or not I went up to my mountain hut. There I found a seventeen-syllable poem written by my father and left in the hut for me. It said:

> Not even an echo
> Responds to my call in the
> Summery mountains.

It gave me a strange feeling to know that even my aged father had been brought down to Lubang.

A lot of newspapers and magazines had been left in the hut, along with a new search-party uniform in a sack, and an old uniform with the name Ichirō Gozen sewn on it. Ichirō Gozen had been in Kainan Middle School when I was there. I examined the old uniform and found that it was torn in several places, and the cuffs had been turned up to make the trousers shorter. The shoulders were particularly worn, and when I reflected that Gozen, who had specialized in judo, had had wider shoulders than any of the other students in our school, I decided that the uniform had really been worn by him.

With a ball-point pen that I had requisitioned from an islander, I penned the following message on the back of a large Red Cross leaflet: "Thank you for the two uniforms and the hat which you kindly left for me. In case you are not sure, let me inform you that I am in good health. Hiroo Onoda, Army Second Lieutenant." Naturally I did not put the date on the message, but to make sure that it would not blow away in the wind before someone found it, I put a small rock on top of it.

I went to a place some distance from the hut and read the newspapers I had found. I learned that a large funeral had been held in Manila for Kozuka. It was written up at considerable length as an example of Japan-Philippine friendship. I could not decide immediately whether this was just talk or not.

I judged that these newspapers, unlike those of 1959, had really been produced in Japan. Still, it puzzled me that they did not contain a word about the war between the East Asia Co-Prosperity League and the United States. Putting that omission together with the failure of the previous papers to mention Kozuka's "thousand-stitch waistband," I decided that the papers must have been printed specially by the Japanese strategic command for the purpose of leaving them in Lubang.

For one thing, the sending of such a large "search party" to survey Lubang suggested to me that a big battle was going on somewhere, and that America was losing. Otherwise, I could not see how the strategic command could afford to lavish so much attention on this little island. If this was indeed the situation, however, the strategic command would not want to send me newspapers telling me about it for fear that I might decide upon reading the good news to come out of the jungle. In a way then, the omission of the news from the doctored newspapers was a sign to me that I should stay put. Of course the Americans were aware of Japan's activities on Lubang, and they would naturally have to reserve military forces to fight in the Philippines when the Japanese attack came.

In sum, my being on Lubang enabled the Japanese strategists to take a number of steps that would otherwise have been impossible. If the cumulative effect were to be that the Americans would keep a number of planes in readiness against a Japanese attack on the Philippines, it was well worth the price of printing a few doctored newspapers to prevent me from showing myself. So long as I remained in place, the larger the "search" operations would be—and the more it would cost the Americans in the long run.

I was not one hundred percent convinced I was right about this. Still, it seemed plausible enough. It was quite possible that the Philippines had grown more pro-Japanese than I thought, even possible that Lubang might have separated from the Philippines and called on the league for help. According to the papers, a big funeral had been held in Manila for Kozuka, and that might indeed mean that relations between the Philippines and Japan were better than I had believed.

I read the newspapers over and over; there were many statements that I found difficult to explain. One way or the other, I convinced myself that it would be best for the time being not to adopt aggressive tactics against the islanders, even though up until now they had acted as stooges for the Americans.

I had pledged to avenge Kozuka's death, but the arrival of the search parties had prevented me from taking action. Now, finally, both search parties were gone, but the idea that Japan and the Philippines had become friendly nations deterred me. In my heart I whispered to Kozuka, "I haven't forgotten you. Just give me a little more time."

The rainy season arrived. For the first time, I had to put up a *bahai* for only myself. Choosing a site below the observation peak near Looc, I made the house smaller and simpler than

30–32. The search party sent by the Japanese government in 1954 included Corporal Shimada's brother Fukuji and my oldest brother Toshio, who was also in the 1959 search party. He is at the right in the pictures above and below. *Left,* the balloon-carried message from the Ministry of Health and Welfare reads, "Hiroo, your brothers are here" (1972).

33–37. *Above*: at left are two messages addressed to Kozuka and me, which we regarded as fake; at right is my father's calligraphy, left in 1972 in one of the message boxes set up by the search party. *Below*, my father, Tanejirō (holding microphone), and Major Taniguchi accompanied the 1972–73 search parties.

Kodansha

Norio Suzuki

38–39. When Norio Suzuki left Japan in 1974, he intended to look for me on Lubang. To prove that there was no trickery involved, he took pictures not only of me but of the two of us together.

Norio Suzuki

Norio Suzuki

Kyodo News Service

40–41. My last night at Wakayama Point was spent with Suzuki and Major Taniguchi. The following morning, before we went down to Brol, my brother Toshio (*below*) and Akihisa Kashiwai came to our camp.

42–43. Philippine troops examine my meager possessions, some of which I had had for thirty years: cooking utensils, bolo knife blades, bottles, hand grenades and assorted ammunition. Before leaving Lubang, I showed Suzuki and the search party where and how I had been living.

44. As a sign of surrender, I gave my sword to President Ferdinand Marcos. He accepted my apologies for my past deeds and returned the sword to me.

45. At Malacañang Palace with Kashiwai, Mrs. Marcos, President Marcos and Toshio

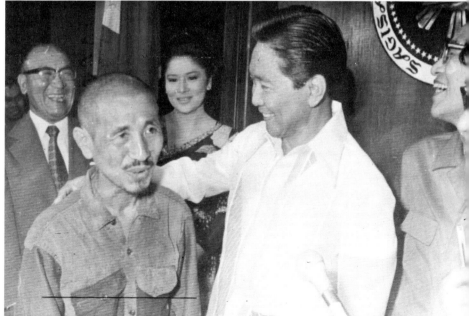

Kyodo News Service

46–47. I returned to Japan on March 12, 1974. At a press interview held after my arrival at 4:30 P.M., my answer to one question was that "the hardest thing of all was to have lost comrades." (*Below left to right*, Suzuki, my mother Tamae, my father Tanezō, myself, Taniguchi and Kashiwai.)

Kyodo News Service

48–49. I spent nineteen days in Tokyo's First National Hospital (*above*), where more than two hundred tests were carried out. The conclusion: both my physical and mental health are far better than Japanese of my age who live in a contemporary urban environment. I returned to Kainan just in time for the cherry blossoms (*right*).

before, but even so it took me two or three times as much
effort as when Kozuka was with me.

Immediately after Kozuka died, I told myself that it would
not be so different living alone, but whenever I settled down in
one spot, I felt the difference acutely. When there were two of
us, Kozuka could go for our water while I cooked. Now I had
to do both chores. And when I went for the water I now had to
carry my rifle with me, even in the rainy season.

Curiously enough, I was less lonely than I had thought I
would be. I simply felt no great urge to talk. Actually, Kozuka
had never been much of a talker, and I myself am not the
sort to take the initiative in conversation.

When I was in the hut, I patched my clothes and repaired
utensils and waited for it to stop raining. When I had nothing
to do, I deliberated about how far I should go along with the
idea of Japanese-Philippine friendship. For the time being, I
intended to avoid trouble with the islanders, but I suspected
at times that this was a mistake. Just before the rainy season I
had seen signs that the islanders were starting to encroach upon
what I regarded as my territory.

If I continued to stay quiet after the rainy season, they might
decide I had lost my nerve, and this would further embolden
those among them who were sympathetic with the enemy.
Should that happen, must I continue to hold off?

I had been carrying on an aggressive campaign against the
islanders for a long time, because I considered that to be my
duty as a guerrilla agent. So far as I could tell, the war was
still going on, and the Filipinos, along with the Americans,
were still enemies. Was I supposed to sit here and be patient
when there were enemies all around me?

Were the Filipinos now really friendly? If they were, then the
islanders on Lubang must be friends. And if the islanders were
now friendly, I would have to change my attitude and my way
of life.

The question that stumped me was how I should go about it. There is a saying that yesterday's enemy is today's friend, but had I not seen my best friend slaughtered before my eyes just six months ago? If Japan and the Philippines were now friendly, why had there been any need to kill Kozuka?

For the first time since coming to this island, I felt that I was reaching a turning point. More and more I sat idly staring at some fixed point and thinking these things over. And as I pondered, I stroked my goatee—the goatee I had started growing when I swore to take revenge for Kozuka's death.

Finally the rainy season ended, and the first anniversary of Kozuka's death grew near. Ordinarily we would have been beginning our beacon raids around this time, but this year I decided against carrying them out. I wanted to avoid unnecessary trouble with the islanders. Anyway, the Japanese strategic command already knew that I was here and in good health. Over and above this, I was afraid that if I sallied forth near the islanders, my yearning for revenge would get the best of me. I kept telling myself that until I made sure how relations between Japan and the Philippines actually were, I should avoid all contact with the islanders.

On the anniversary of Kozuka's slaying, I stood alone in the deep jungle and prayed for his eternal happiness. I wanted to go and make a deep bow before that large tombstone, but if I did, I could not avoid seeing the islanders harvesting their rice, as they had been harvesting it a year ago. I would go some other day.

In late November I visited the mountain hut for the first time in a long time. There was no new information from the strategic command, although I thought it was about time for some secret message to arrive. The only items of interest in the hut were a leaflet written by my younger brother Shigeo, a special Lubang issue of a journal put out by the alumni of the Nakano School, and a note from someone claiming to be an official of the Japanese Ministry of Health and Welfare. The note said, "I was in Mindoro collecting the remains of Japanese troops who died there. It is now half a year since the search parties were called off. I decided to come and see how you were."

The fact that the man from the Ministry of Health and Welfare had come indicated to me that my message acknowledging the receipt of the uniforms had been found, but there was nothing in the note about it, nor could I find any comment about it in the alumni group's magazine.

I took this latter to mean that the strategic command was not putting out information about me for the general public. Just as they had suppressed the information about Kozuka's waistband, they were saying nothing in public about the message I had written. The war was still going on after all. There was nothing to do but wait for a further communication.

A new year arrived, and for the twenty-ninth time I celebrated New Year's Day on Lubang.

FEBRUARY 20, 1974

Wakayama Point was at the confluence of two rivers. There were many *nanka* trees near it, and about three hundred yards downstream, there was a banana field. This was one of the best places on the island for gathering food, but the police knew that, and there were frequent patrols.

On February 16, 1974, I went to a slope from which I could look down on the point. Besides the Japanese flag that had been raised by the search party last year, I saw another, newer Japanese flag.

"I guess they've come again," I grumbled. "Well, let them come!"

Then I saw somebody in the shadow of a tree. I could not tell whether it was an islander, a policeman or a member of a Japanese search party.

Almost simultaneously I heard voices nearby. About ten islanders who had been up in the mountains cutting trees were running down the slope. I was sure they had spotted me. I crossed the river and hid in the *bosa* trees on the opposite slope. For a while I stayed there holding my breath; then I looked out. There was no one in sight, so I decided to move to a spot above the banana field where I could see anyone approaching Wakayama Point. Two men carrying guns came and went, but nothing else happened that called for alarm.

I stayed in the same place for three days, and then my food gave out. Turning my hat and jacket inside out, I covered them with a camouflage of twigs and leaves. I was planning to go nearer the point and pick some *nanka*.

When the sun began to set, I crept silently toward the *nanka* grove. When I was nearly there I spotted something large and white next to the river. Squinting at it for a time, I made it out to be a mosquito net. It seemed to be big enough for two, and I was sure I had stumbled across a couple of policemen camping out.

This was more than I could take. They were camping on my territory, between me and the food I needed, and I resolved to attack them. It would have to be a surprise attack, but if I knocked out one of them at the beginning, the rest would be man-to-man combat, which I was confident I would win. I released the safety lock on my rifle.

Going forward five or six paces, I sighted a man with his back to the river. He was building a fire, obviously to cook his dinner. After ascertaining that there was no gun nearby, I called out to him.

He stood up and turned around. His eyes were round, and he wore a T-shirt, dark blue trousers and rubber sandals, He faced me and saluted. Then he saluted again. His hands were trembling, and I would have sworn his knees were too.

The islanders almost always fled the minute I called out to them, but this man stood his ground. True, he was shaking, but he was also making a proper salute. It flashed through my mind that he might be the son of a soldier in the Japanese occupation force.

He opened his mouth and stammered, "I'm Japanese. I'm Japanese."

He said this two or three more times in a high-pitched voice. My first thought was that he was a Japanese-speaking Filipino, and that the police had put him on to me. I quickly looked around to see if I had walked into a trap. There must be another one somewhere.

Keeping my rifle ready, I asked, "Did you come from the Japanese government?"

"No."

"Are you from the Youth Foreign Cooperation Society?"

"No."

"Well, who are you?"

"I'm only a tourist."

Tourist? What could he mean by that? Why would a tourist come to this island? There was something fishy about this character, and I was fairly sure he had been sent by the enemy.

He asked, "Are you Onoda-san?"

"Yes, I'm Onoda."

"Really, Lieutenant Onoda?"

I nodded, and he went on.

"I know you've had a long, hard time. The war's over. Won't you come back to Japan with me?"

His use of polite Japanese expressions convinced me that he must have been brought up in Japan, but he was rushing things too much. Did he think that he could just make the simple statement that the war was over, and I would go running back to Japan with him? After all these years, it made me angry.

"No, I won't go back! For me, the war hasn't ended!"

"Why?"

"You wouldn't understand. If you want me to go back to Japan, bring me my orders. There must be proper orders!"

"What do you plan to do? Die here?"

"I will if I don't have any orders to the contrary."

I said this gruffly and straight to his face. This was my first meeting with Norio Suzuki.

If he had not been wearing socks, I might have shot him. At the very least, I would not have let him take my photograph.

But he had on these thick woolen socks even though he was wearing rubber sandals. The islanders would never do anything so incongruous. The ones who could afford to wear socks would have had on shoes too. I came to the conclusion that the young man must really be Japanese.

He offered me a Marlboro cigarette, and I took it. It was the first foreign cigarette I had had for a long time. Still, I remained suspicious.

When he said he would like to talk, I replied, "In that case, let's go someplace else. It's dangerous for me to stand around like this in the open for a long time. Come on over into that clump of trees."

"Wait a minute," he said.

He reached into his rucksack and pulled out a novel, which he gave to me. I put it in the large pocket of my trousers.

"I'll go first," I said, or rather commanded.

It was not simply a case of not wanting to stand here long enough for the enemy to surround me. Any minute an islander might happen by on his way up the river to fish. The young man hurriedly grabbed his camera and flash attachment, then put out his hand to pick up his bolo knife but thought better of it and stopped midway.

We went across a rice field and started up the slope on the north. As we climbed, the young man said, "If I tell the embassy that I met you, they won't believe me. Will you let me take a photograph for proof?"

Pointing to his flash attachment, he added, "This will make light."

I answered, "It ought to. It's a flashbulb."

"Oh, you know about flashbulbs?" He seemed surprised.

We went about fifty yards farther, then sat down. It was dark now.

The young man said, "Onoda-san, the emperor and the people of Japan are worried about you."

"Did you bring any orders for me?"

"No."

"In that case, they'll have to keep on worrying."

He started telling me how Japan had lost the war and had been at peace for many years. What he said corresponded perfectly with what I had long regarded as enemy propaganda and was completely different from the way I had sized things up myself. If what he was saying was true, I would have to change my way of thinking. This idea upset me, and I remained silent.

Breaking off, he said, "Let me take a picture."

I consented. It was a gamble on my part. I knew by now that the young man was Japanese, but I was not sure what his real aim was. Still, if I let him take my picture, there ought to be some sort of reaction before long.

He trained his flashlight on his camera and put on the flash attachment. After taking two shots, he still seemed dissatisfied.

"I'm not too confident about these flashbulb shots. If you don't mind, I'd like to take a daylight shot tomorrow. About three in the afternoon would be a good time, if you're willing to come."

That gave me a turn. Was he a fraud after all? With that expensive camera and flash equipment, why should he be worried about the results?

"I don't want to do that," I replied casually. I was trying to think of some way to make him give himself away. The first step, I supposed, was to ask him a few questions.

"You didn't tell me your name," I remarked.

"My name is Norio Suzuki."

"How do you write 'Norio'? With the character in 'rule'?"

"No, with the character *ki* that means 'annals.'"

"Oh. You mean the *ki* in Kii Peninsula, don't you?"

"That's right."

So far I was getting nowhere. Before I could think of anything else to ask, he started questioning me about life on the island and how Kozuka and Shimada had died and a lot of other things. In the course of the conversation I referred to something that had happened in Japan recently.

Startled, he inquired, "How did you know about that?"

"I have a transistor radio," I replied nonchalantly.

That really surprised him. He listened with open mouth as I told him how we had acquired the radio. I, for my part, kept watching his reactions closely for any sign that he might not be what he said he was. I had not talked with anybody since Kozuka's death sixteen months earlier, and I would have been enjoying myself but for the lingering fear that Norio Suzuki was an enemy agent.

After we talked about two hours, he asked, "What could I do to persuade you to come out of the jungle?"

"Just what it says in the newspapers," I answered. "Major Taniguchi is my immediate superior. I won't give in until I have direct orders from him."

Major Taniguchi was not, in fact, my immediate superior, but I had read in one of the newspapers left by the search party that Major Taniguchi had said he was. This meant that Major Taniguchi was no longer involved with army secrets. What I could not understand was why, if the war was really over, Major Taniguchi did not offer some explanation that made sense or send me some sort of written message. If, on the other hand, the war was still going on, why did I not receive new orders of some kind?

In any case, without positive proof that Norio Suzuki was not an enemy agent, I could not mention the name of my real commander, Lieutenant General Yokoyama, or even that of Major Takahashi. In short, the only name I could mention was that of Major Taniguchi.

"Let me get this straight then," said Suzuki. "If I bring Major Taniguchi, and if Major Taniguchi tells you to come to

such and such a place at such and such a time, you will come,
right?"

"Right."

Needless to say, when the time came, I intended to make sure
I was dealing with the real Major Taniguchi, but there seemed
to be no point in bringing this up now.

By way of testing my newfound friend, I said, "Why don't I
go with you to your camp and stay with you? Then you can
take your picture in the morning."

My real object was to keep him under guard until morning.
That meant staying awake all night, but that was just part of
my work. Anyway, the idea excited me a little.

Arriving back in front of his mosquito net, I sat down on the
sand, put my pack beside me, and laid my rifle on it. The
wind had died down, and the night was dark.

From his rucksack, Suzuki got a fresh pack of cigarettes, a
can of sweetened beans and a bottle of gin. He offered me a drink,
which I refused.

"I tried drinking when I was in China," I told him, "but I
didn't like it."

"Too bad," he said. "I was hoping we could sit here and
talk over a couple of drinks."

He seemed so disappointed that I said, "I'll have some of the
beans instead. I like sweets."

He started sipping his drink, but noticing that I had no
spoon for the beans, darted into the mosquito net and brought
one out, sticking it into the open can. I took a spoonful in my
mouth and savored the wonderful flavor. I felt that for the
first time in thirty years I was eating something fit for human
beings. My tongue, my whole mouth, melted.

Suzuki said, "I'm lucky. I never dreamed I would meet you
after only four days here."

Puffing on my cigarette, I looked up at the moonless sky. This was the first time I had ever sat in such an open place so long, even on very dark nights.

I answered his questions about my food, the weather on Lubang and the islanders. I even told him about my life in Hankow and my experience in the army before I came to Lubang. I jumped from one subject to another and digressed a number of times, but that did not seem to bother Suzuki. What I was really trying to do was try to find out something about him—what kind of person he was. He, for his part, seemed to grow sleepy from the gin, which he finished off, but from time to time he would open his half-closed eyes and ask another question.

"If you're sleepy," I said, "go to bed. I'll stay here by you until the sun is high enough for you to take your picture."

He straightened up and began telling me about himself. He said he had wandered about all over the world, working his way through about fifty countries in four years. I thought to myself, somewhat admiringly, that he looked like the type who might do something like that. He reminded me a little of myself in those erratic days before I went into the army. I felt myself drawn to him to some extent.

Later he wrote somewhere that I had talked all night without interruption. Although I will admit that I talked a lot, it was not because I was fascinated with the sound of my own voice. In the hope of eliciting some sort of reaction or information from him, I fed him a wide selection of facts that it would do no harm for him to know. But when he asked how many bullets I had, I flatly refused to answer.

Eventually he stood up and said, "I'm hungry. Let's cook some food." He started over to the river to get water, and I took the precaution of going with him.

When he took out his mess kit, my suspicions were suddenly reawakened. It was of the type that American soldiers carried.

I was further alarmed when he plucked some leaves off a nearby tree and said, "Let's put some of these in for flavor."

He explained that he had learned this from the Lubang islanders. Although I had been on the island for thirty years, I had never watched the islanders preparing food, nor had I ever seen leaves in the pots they left behind in the mountains. I did not even know the leaves were edible. I also found it odd that he put in a flavoring made by pickling in salt a small fish found around the island. I knew the islanders ate this, but would a tourist who had been here only four days know about it?

I considered both the leaves and the seasoning ample reason for suspicion, and when he served the food, I was careful not to pick up my chopsticks until after had had started eating.

He disarmed me somewhat by saying, "It never occurred to me that I might one day be sitting here with you eating from the same pan. I am honored."

As he was making coffee, the wind came up again. There was not enough wood on the fire, and the smoke blew off into the distance. We picked up some pieces of bamboo that were lying around and put them on the fire, but the smoke continued to rise up toward the clear sky and then blow off toward the river. Not having for years dared build a fire without keeping the smoke to a minimum, I could not help feeling uneasy. When we finished our coffee, I said, "Let's go to the mountains."

As he hurried to get his camera, he pulled three or four photos from his rucksack and handed them to me.

"Do you like nude photos?" he asked. His tone sounded as though he thought I had never seen one before.

I laughed and told him I was not interested. I also gave him back the novel he had given me the night before. This was hardly the time to take up reading as a pastime, even though it was a novel about samurais and the samurai spirit. Strange as it may sound, most of the time I was too busy to read.

Going ahead of him, I climbed up to a place somewhat higher than the place where I had camouflaged myself the evening before. I sat down in a spot from which I could look down on the river, removed the leaves and twigs from my hat and jacket, and turned the clothing right side out. After putting my jacket back on, I rolled up the left sleeve and held up my arm so that Suzuki could see the scar there.

"This," I told him, "is what they call my 'distinguishing mark.' Make sure that it and the chrysanthemum emblem on my rifle show up in the picture."

The scar was from a wound I had received in middle school. While we were practicing *kendō*, my opponent's bamboo sword had broken and pierced my arm. My brothers and nearly all of my middle school friends would recognize the scar.

Turning my rifle sideways, I laid it across my knees. Suzuki focused his camera and took several shots. Assuming that he was finished, I started to leave. I could see no purpose in staying any longer.

But Suzuki said, "Wait just a minute. If I don't take a picture of the two of us together, people might think I faked the shots."

Squatting beside me, Suzuki said, "Let me hold the rifle."

I did as he requested. I did not know whether he was a friend or not, but I was pretty sure by this time that he was not an enemy.

When the picture was taken, he said, "Don't you want to see cherry blossoms again? Wouldn't you like to see Mount Fuji?"

Without answering these questions, I said, "I am fifty-two years old, but physically I don't think I am more than thirty-seven or thirty-eight. So long as my body is healthy, I am strong enough mentally not to do anything to destroy my own life."

"Onoda-san," he said seriously, "if there are official orders

from your superior, you really will come out, won't you?
You're not joking, are you? If I name the time and the place,
will you really come?"

"Yes," I replied rather impatiently, "I'll come. If you say so,
I'll come."

Since last night, I had told Suzuki everything I had to say.
Even if he should turn out after all to be an enemy, I felt sure
that one way or another my message would reach Japan, and
that my description of the death of Shimada and Kozuka
would be relayed to their families.

I was relieved to have that off my chest. I myself might
still be killed by an enemy agent or die alone of illness, but I
could do so now without regrets. I also felt more cheerful for
having been able to talk to someone in Japanese after so many
months of solitude.

"I'll come back for you as soon as I can," said Suzuki. "The
press will make a huge story out of this. You won't believe it!"

He laughed and then saluted. I nodded and shook his hand.
He was genuinely happy, and I thought he had a good, honest
face.

I said good-bye and shouldering my pack started walking
toward the mountains. The sun was high now; it was getting
hotter. I quickened my pace. Suzuki might have an honest
face, but if in spite of everything he was working for the enemy,
I had better move as far away as possible before he had a
chance to report.

A little farther on I saw three or four islanders cutting trees.
I crossed the valley and hid in the bushes on the opposite
slope. Already I had ceased to put much store by Suzuki's
parting remarks. I thought of Kozuka, who had often said,
"Let's wait for the people to come for us, but let's not depend
on it."

The next morning I went over to Snake Mountain to check on the ammunition that I had hidden there.

It was my intention to hold out on this island, if necessary, for twenty years more. As I had told Suzuki, I considered my body to be no more than thirty-seven or thirty-eight years old. I was confident that I could last another twenty years.

The main reason for checking on the ammunition was to make sure I would not lose track of its exact location. I also wanted, however, to check on the number of bullets left, divide the number by twenty, and determine how many I could use per year.

During the early years, I had used about sixty rounds a year, but in the years just before Kozuka died, this number had fallen to only about twenty. Now that I was alone, I might have to use more in case I encountered enemy patrols, but I hoped that I would be able to hold the number down to no more than forty or fifty a year.

Having counted the bullets, I put one third of them aside as reserve ammunition, in case some unforeseen need should arise. Dividing the number of the remaining bullets by twenty, I found that I could use thirty bullets a year. I decided that I would just have to make do on that.

About ten months had gone by now since the departure of the search parties in which my family and friends had participated. I had expected a friendly army to land at almost any time, but there had been no further word. I was beginning to think that the plans had been changed.

That, I thought, was all right too. If ever I did manage to return to Japan, I would still have to work and sweat every day, and I could do that just as well on Lubang. Staying here even had one advantage: if I died, it would be death in the line of duty, and my spirit would be enshrined at Yasukuni Shrine. That idea appealed to me.

Before allowing Suzuki to photograph me, I had said to him,

"You apparently risked your life to come to this island. Now it is my turn to gamble."

I did not really believe what he said about the war being over. In several instances, his account agreed with what I had heard over the radio and read in the newspapers, but I still saw inexplicable discrepancies. If the war was really over, why would such a large search party as the last be sent to Lubang? Why would they call themselves a "search party" when their purpose was to survey the island? Wasn't this survey proof that Lubang was considered very important from the strategic viewpoint?

Surely the war between America and the East Asia Co-Property League was continuing, and as long as it continued, I could not neglect my duties for a single day. Until some new secret orders arrived, I intended to fight to preserve the territory I was "occupying."

Still, I found that I could not completely ignore Suzuki's explanation of how things were. Ninety-nine percent was unbelievable, and I was in doubt about that remaining one percent. It was actually on that one percent that I was betting when I let Suzuki take my picture. If the war was really over, as he said, then he would immediately tell Major Taniguchi about his meeting with me, and Major Taniguchi would send word of some sort to me.

But I was sure that this would not happen. Major Taniguchi knew perfectly well the nature of the orders under which I had come to Lubang, and he knew that I could not leave the island unless those orders were properly rescinded.

That was the key point. The strategic command had not rescinded my orders; that meant simply that they wanted me to stay on the island.

According to the newspapers, Major Taniguchi was now a bookdealer living in Miyazaki Prefecture. I suspected, however, that this was merely for public consumption, and that in fact he was still a secret agent, disguised as a civilian. It is not so easy for people engaged in secret warfare to return to civilian life.

Moreover, if the war had really ended thirty years ago, why should Major Taniguchi's name come up only at this late date? Why could he not have issued new orders to me in his own name much earlier? The fact that he had not done so seemed to me proof that all this time he too had still been engaged in secret warfare. No doubt he had been given some new assignment that entailed his pretending to be an ordinary citizen.

True, thirty years had gone by, and it was unlikely that the Sugi Brigade of which I had been a member had continued on unaltered. Still, when the new army took over, the rolls and records of the old army would naturally have passed to it, and they must know my name and whereabouts.

Well, I had rolled my dice on that one percent. The only thing to do now was wait and see—without depending too much on the results.

When I finished counting the bullets, I started out on my usual patrol route. I could not afford to consider the meeting with Suzuki as anything more than an unexpected diversion.

LUBANG, SAYONARA

I almost never dreamed, and when I did, it was almost always the same dream.

I would be defending myself against an enemy patrol that had spotted me. Bullets were whizzing by me, and I was returning fire from behind a shelter of some sort. I would aim and pull the trigger, but the gun would not go off. Was it a bad cartridge, or was the gun not working properly? I would pull the trigger again, and again the gun would not fire. By this time the enemy's bullets were nearly grazing my ears. One more try. Still no luck. The gun was broken. . . .

At this point, I always woke up.

In March I began to have a different dream, and a stranger one.

I dreamed I was awakened by a noise and started to ask Kozuka if he had heard it too. But Kozuka was not there, and I wondered where he was. Then I awoke and realized I had been dreaming. Kozuka was not there because he was dead. Only after this did I really wake up. It was a dream within a dream.

Kozuka would not appear even in a dream within a dream. Nothing made me feel more alone than that idea.

On March 5, near the mountain hut, I heard the excited voices of islanders. I wondered what they were doing so deep in the mountains.

Suddenly it occurred to me that maybe Suzuki had come

back to the island. About two weeks had passed, plenty of time for him to go to Japan and back. I had given him my word, and I thought I ought at least to go and see whether he had come. If he had, it would not be right to let him down. He had been so elated and so earnest when he had promised to come again.

I went to the mountain hut, but saw no change. I decided that the excited cries I had heard meant nothing more than that the natives had caught a water buffalo. I had no objection to that. Let them be! I had a two-day food supply, and I did not plan to leave until I had eaten it. I spent the night on a nearby slope.

Two mornings later I remembered that Suzuki and I had agreed to leave messages in a box that had been set up by search parties on a boulder at Snake Mountain. Maybe I would find a message there. At dusk, I went to see.

A brand new plastic bag was taped to the side of the box; I knew he must have come back. I thought of Suzuki's friendly, honest face and decided that maybe I had been wrong to doubt him.

In the bag were two of the photos he had taken as proof and a noted saying, "I've come back for you, just as I promised." There were also copies of two army orders.

The minute I looked at the photos, which had been enlarged to eight by ten size, I was struck by my resemblance to my uncles on both sides of the family. It also seemed to me that I looked rather like generals Sadao Araki and Senjūrō Hayashi, and it occurred to me that if a man stayed in the army that long, maybe he could not help looking like that. This was the first time in thirty years that I had seen my face as anything other than a reflection in a river.

One order was from Fourteenth Area Army headquarters and the other from the Special Squadron. The first, issued in the name of General Yamashita, was the same as the order reproduced in leaflets dropped by search parties. The other, however, said that "instructions would be given to Lieutenant Onoda orally."

Oral instructions! This was what I had been waiting for all these years. To men in special units like mine, there were always direct oral orders in addition to the usual printed ones. Otherwise, it would have been impossible to maintain secrecy.

Apparently Major Taniguchi had been sent to deliver my oral orders.

I laid my plans. The aerial distance from Snake Mountain to Wakayama Point was no more than about six miles, but the route involved crossing several mountains and valleys. The trip would take eight or nine hours of walking, but I decided to allow myself two days. For fear of running into islanders, I could only walk in the early morning and late evening, and I did not want to try to advance too rapidly, because haste tends to make a person careless about his surroundings.

That evening as I rested at Shingu Point, I asked myself what the oral orders would be. They might, of course, be simply to stay on Lubang and continue fighting. Or they might tell me to shift to a completely new location. Considering that so many people had come the year before to survey the island, it seemed possible that the strategic command now knew all it wanted to know and might completely relieve me of my duties. The only certainty was that if they were oral orders, they were secret.

"The time has come," I said to myself, "to take a chance."

Whatever the content of the orders, I must go and receive them. But there remained the possibility that all of this was the work of the enemy. Or maybe real orders were on the way, but the enemy had found out about them and was striking first. Still there is never an end to doubts. If you doubt everything, you end up not being able to do anything, and certainly it was high time that new orders be sent to me! My only hestitation was that after carrying on for thirty years, I did not want to let everything go down the drain because of some false step on my part. I had to be careful still!

Presumably Major Taniguchi had come because I had mentioned his name to Suzuki, but it was really General Yokoyama who had given me my orders and Major Takahashi who had instructed me to proceed to Lubang. Any new oral orders should properly come from General Yokoyama, but I supposed that headquarters in Japan had picked Major Taniguchi as a substitute because he was familiar with the situation. Major Taniguchi might be posing as a bookdealer, but in reality he was still a secret warfare agent.

True, I would not know until I saw the man whether he was really Major Taniguchi or not. The plain fact was that I might be walking into an enemy trap, and if I did not exercise the utmost care, I could end up being shot in the back. I must be as cautious as possible and at the same time be prepared to shoot my way out if I should suddenly find myself surrounded.

It rained on the second day of my journey. When the rain let up in the evening, I started walking again, but I was soon drenched by the water falling from the trees. It was about the same as walking in the rain.

The next day Major Taniguchi delivered to me orally my orders from the Special Section of the Chief of Staff's Headquarters.

Outside the tent it was daylight, the first morning in thirty years with no duties to carry out.

Young Suzuki arose and asked whether he should now let the others know of my arrival.

"Not now," said the Major. "Let's take our time and eat first."

Major Taniguchi and I went to the Agcawayan River to wash up. He handed me a razor and suggested that I shave.

"I'll shave off my goatee," I said. "I don't need it to scare the islanders anymore."

"No," said the Major. "Leave that, because the president specifically requested that you come as you were in the mountains."

"President?"

"Yes, President Marcos of the Philippines said he wanted to see you after you were found."

Major Taniguchi shaved the back of my neck for me and then handed me some face lotion.

"Being down here, you wouldn't know it, but you'll be a celebrity when you return to Japan. You will have to make appearances all over the country. You may as well start now getting used to cosmetics."

For the first time, he laughed. I could not understand at first what he meant about my having to go all over the country. But I applied the lotion to my face anyway. It had a fragrance that I had not smelled since I left Hankow, more than thirty years ago.

Major Taniguchi went back to the tent ahead of me, and I stripped down to my loincloth so that I could wash my clothes. I could not use soap on them, because it would wash away the carbon from cooking pots with which I had dyed them. I just rinsed everything in water to get the sweat out.

When the washing was done, I stood there looking at the river for a time, and then I looked up at the sun. Whenever I had crossed this river in the past, I had first looked carefully in all directions, then darted across the river and into a clump of *bosa* trees. Now I was standing here practically naked with the sunlight streaming down on me. It was an odd feeling.

What was to happen now? Major Taniguchi had said that I could go back to Japan immediately, but the idea of going back and trying to live among ordinary people frightened me. I could not quite imagine it.

When I had flown out of the Utsunomiya airport on that
night so many years ago, I had discarded all my personal hopes
for the future. I told myself at the time that I must put all that
behind me. After that, whenever I started to think of home or
my family, I deliberately forced the thoughts out of my mind.
This became a matter of habit, and eventually the thoughts
stopped coming. For more than twenty years now, the idea
of home had barely occurred to me, and I had never once
dreamed of my family. My military assignment was my life
and my support.

Now that life was ending, and that support had been abruptly
removed. As I looked at the thick clump of trees across the
river, my brother Tadao's face floated up before me.

I thought, "Maybe I should go to Brazil, where Tadao lives,
and become a farmer. After all, I'm used to the jungle . . . One
of those leaflets said Tadao has six children. He only had two
thirty years ago when I left Japan."

For the first time, I began to feel the weight of those thirty
years, but my reverie went on.

"Maybe Tadao would let me adopt one of his boys. If I
had one grown boy to help me in the fields . . ."

I finished wringing out the clothes and took them back to
the tent, still clad only in my loincloth. This was the first time
I had done anything like that in all the years on Lubang, and
it made me nervous. I hurried along, taking long strides.

Handing me some new underwear, Major Taniguchi said,
"My wife sent this for you."

I put it on immediately. Suzuki mischievously took a picture
of me while I was changing from my loincloth to my new
shorts, but I was happy to find later that the picture did not
come out.

The three of us breakfasted on red rice, fish and stewed vegetables, all from cans. We ate ravenously.

Suzuki lighted a beacon signaling to the others that I was

here; two hours later the contingent from Brol arrived at Wakayama Point. Among them was my oldest brother Toshio. He put both hands on my shoulders and said, "We finally found you!" This was our reunion after thirty years.

The road leading down to Brol was barely wide enough for two men, but Colonel Los Panios (district commander) and Lieutenant Colonel Pawan (commander of the radar base) insisted on walking on either side of me.

I changed into a suit my brother had brought me and was given a camera to carry in my left hand. Without asking, I understood why we had to walk three abreast on the narrow road: there was a possibility that one of the islanders might take a shot at me. After all, they had reason to hate me.

The two officers kept a sharp lookout to right and left. At times they walked before and behind me; at others. we were shoulder to shoulder. I was grateful for their solicitude, but deep down I would not have minded being shot.

When we entered the town of Brol, there were Philippine soldiers with automatics lined up along the street at intervals of about ten yards. Despite these security precautions, when we stopped to rest at the mayor's house, the islanders who looked in through the windows registered nothing but curiosity on their faces. I saw no signs of anger.

After we had had some soft drinks, we started out for Snake Mountain to get Kozuka's rifle and my sword. When we came out of the house, we found that several hundred islanders had assembled on the main street. They were all laughing, and some were waving at us. There was not an unfriendly face among them. My brother was vastly relieved.

When I first came to Lubang, Brol consisted of nothing but fifteen or sixteen nipa houses. Now there must be about a hundred houses. Once again I felt my years.

I started climbing Snake Mountain at my usual pace, but Major Taniguchi, Suzuki and the Philippine troops with us soon fell behind. I had to stop and wait for them to catch up.

Major Taniguchi laughed and said, "When Onoda says 'thirty yards,' he means 'three hundred yards.' "

From crevices between the rocks in a cave, I took out the rifle, the sword, and the dagger that I had received from my mother. By this time the sun had set.

We started back with the aid of Lieutenant Colonel Pawan's flashlight, but it was so dark that we stopped and made a torch out of palm leaves. Major Taniguchi and I walked together under its light. We all got wet to the shins in the river.

At the guardhouse of the radar base, I changed into my old clothes to comply with President Marcos's request. As a "prisoner" who had in accordance with orders admitted defeat, I was in no position to object. I simply did as I was told.

Philippine troops were lined up at attention on both sides of the asphalt road in the base. They saluted me by presenting arms. Saluted *me*, if you can believe it, when I was nothing more than a prisoner of war. I was astounded.

The place was lit up like daylight. Taking my sword, wrapped in a white cloth, in my left hand, I advanced toward Major General Rancudo. After saluting him, I held up the sword with both hands and presented it to him. He took it from me briefly as a token of acceptance, then handed it back to me immediately. For a moment something that might be called the pride of a samurai swept over me.

I remembered how Kozuka, looking down on this radar base from a distance, had once said, "We'll take that over someday, won't we?"

But how strange it was to be received here like a triumphant general! Having seen the attention given by the Japanese newspapers to Kozuka's death, I suddenly realized that they must also be raising quite a stir over me.

"I mustn't disappoint them," I thought. "My uniform may be a mess, but I will try to look like a soldier."

And I marched as firmly and proudly as I could, putting strength into every step.

That night in a room in the officers' quarters, I drew charts showing where I had hidden my ammunition and extra clothing, so that the people from the Ministry of Health and Welfare could find them later. As I drew the charts, I laughed ruefully to think that all my dreams had ended as a dream.

My dream had been to make a bastion of Lubang. The port at Tilik could be an atomic submarine base or something like that, and I would develop the mountainous areas in my own way. We would plant more palms, and make more paddy fields, and raise more cows. The island would become a self-sufficient, impregnable stronghold.

"Aren't you sleepy yet?" called my brother.

"Not quite yet," I answered.

Although we had been reunited after thirty years, I had not yet talked with him very much. When I finished drawing my charts, I looked up at him. He seemed to have been staring at my profile. He was blinking sheepishly.

The next day I went to Kozuka's grave. After burning incense before the tombstone, I knelt in silent prayer. With my eyes closed, I saw Kozuka on the hill, screaming "It's my chest!" and falling over. I also saw Shimada falling at Gontin.

"Both of you, forgive me," I begged. "I've let you down."

In my ears echoed the sound of their voices.

"Lieutenant, let's wait but . . . let's not depend on it," Kozuka had said.

And Shimada, looking at the picture of his wife and daughter: "She must be about the age to start liking boys."

We had never talked about it, but we all had hoped that we would someday return to Japan together.

And now I alone was returning, leaving the spirits of my

two irreplaceable comrades on this island. Returning to a Japan that had lost the war thirty years earlier. Returning to my fatherland for which I had fought until the day before. If there had not been people around, I would have beat my head on the ground and wailed.

Ten minutes later the helicopter I had boarded rose off Lubang, flailing the grass around it. Through the windproof glass I could see Kozuka's grave, and gradually the whole island, grow smaller and begin to fade.

For the first time, I was looking down upon my battlefield.

Why had I fought here for thirty years? Who had I been fighting for? What was the cause?

Manila Bay was bathed in the evening sun.

Lubang

Tagbac

Malik

Vigo R.

Vigo

Tilik

Kozuka H

Tomibo

Ambulong

Filik Mt.

Snake Mt.   Ramano
                   Point

✗ Five Hundred
  (Radar Base)

Shingu Point

Binacas

Six Hundred

One House Point ✗ Gontin

Lo
Lo

Kainan Point ✗
             Looc

0   1   2   3   4 Miles